Anonymus

Streets Ballads, Popular Poetry and Household Songs of Ireland

Anonymus

Streets Ballads, Popular Poetry and Household Songs of Ireland

ISBN/EAN: 9783741164965

Manufactured in Europe, USA, Canada, Australia, Japa

Cover: Foto ©Angelika Wolter / pixelio.de

Manufactured and distributed by brebook publishing software
(www.brebook.com)

Anonymus

Streets Ballads, Popular Poetry and Household Songs of Ireland

STREET BALLADS,
POPULAR POETRY,

AND

HOUSEHOLD SONGS

OF

IRELAND.

"With hope for our country,
Ye come to us ever, Sweet Songs of our Land."
FRANCES BROWNE.

DUBLIN:
M'GLASHAN AND GILL,
50, UPPER SACKVILLE-ST.
1864.

STREET BALLADS,
POPULAR POETRY,
AND
HOUSEHOLD SONGS.

"*Duke*—O fellow, come, the song we had last night:
Mark it, Cesario; it is old and plain:
The spinsters and the knitters in the sun,
And the free maids that weave their threads with bones,
Do use to chant it: it is silly, sooth,
And dallies with the innocence of love,
Like the old age.

  Clown—Are you ready, Sir?
  Duke—Ay; pr'ythee, sing."

SHAKESPEARE.

To

THE INDUSTRIOUS, HARD-WORKING;

YET CHEERFUL AND GENEROUS:

TO THE PATIENT, LONG-SUFFERING;

YET HOPEFUL AND ASPIRING:

TO THE VIRTUOUS, DEVOTIONAL AND HEROIC:

TO THE PEOPLE OF IRELAND,

AT HOME AND ABROAD,

THIS LITTLE VOLUME IS DEDICATED

BY

THE EDITOR

PREFACE.

A LENGTHENED preface to a Little Book, were as vexatious, and not so interesting, as the frequently repeated protestations and apologies of a parlour-vocalist; or as much out of place as a long-drawn grace, to a light repast, set before children who are blessed with healthy appetites. Thereupon my introduction of myself and my book shall be brief; it is this:

For the past few years the gathering together of these materials has been the occasional amusement of my leisure moments. But it has been more than this: it has been a labour of duty and of love. For I could not rest satisfied to think that these ballads, songs, and poems, which, for the most part, had found a place in my heart from the moment I had cast my eyes upon them, should not be bound together and placed in an accessible form within the reach of the people whom I love, and whom I long to serve in some humble way, commensurate with my poor abilities. That which I could do, I have done; and would stimulate those who can do more, to more profitable work for the Dear Old Land.

Not that I would undervalue the work here attempted to be accomplished. To soothe the resting hour of a labourer amid the prairies and savannahs of the Western world; or to cheer the reposing soldier amid the camp-fires of the bivouac; to sing to the listening ears of Age, the songs of memory and of hope; to Youth the song of love; to Manhood and Womanhood that of patriotism and duty; to the Child the strain which he may not forget, and which may win him to his home, should he stray, and bind him to Ireland in weal or woe: this is a deed, which cannot save a nation from martyrdom, but yet it pours the precious balm of love upon its weary feet, and cheers the hearts of those who may be capable of serving her more than words or songs.

Sept. 20*th*, 1864.

ALPHABETICAL INDEX.

A
	Page
April 20th, 1864	20
A Fragment of M'Aulliffe's Prophecy	58
A Snow Song	60
At Niagara	62
A Picture of Munster	87
A Portrait	91
A Cushla Gal Mo Chree	100
An Exile's Dreams	116
Arthur M'Coy	175
An Cailin Deas	179
A Landlaw Rhyme	191
After the Clare Election	207
A True Story, called "Molly Bawn"	209
A Wail	241
An Irish Mother's Dream	261

B
	Page
Boatman's Hymn	86
Burning of an Emigrant Ship	96
By Memory Inspired	98
Brosna's Banks	153
Blarney Groves	160

C
	Page
Caoch the Piper	23
Connor's Revenge	48
Come to me, Dearest	78
Caitlin Tirrial	198

D
	Page
Dirge for Devin Reily	9
Dirge of Rory O'More	44
Drimin Donn Dilis	132
Davis	199
Drahereen O Machree	205
Dirge of Oilfeir Gras	242

F
	Page
Florence my Child	33
Fineen the Rover	143
Farewell to Pleasant Erinn	225
Fairies	245

G
	Page
Glenflesk	227
Gentle Brideen	237

H
	Page
He built me a light boat	194

I
	Page
Irish Lullaby	15
I'm very happy where I am	176

L
	Page
Lament of the Ejected Irish Peasant	102
Love in the Country	115
Love Ballad	163
Lower Glanmire	211

M
	Page
Mo Cailin Donn	76
Music, Music; come, oh come	109
Mac Kenna's Dream	149
Mo Bhuachaillin Bhan	172
Music in the Street	181
Michael Dwyer	222
My Violon	252
Mallow	267

N
	Page
Nano Nagle	216
Nanny's Sailor Lad	240

O

	Page
Our Olden Tongue	29
Oh, Fair shines the sun on Glenara	77
Owen Reily	140
Oscar, the Dog of Shaun Desmond	185
On the Bay	258
Over the Morning Dew	269

P

Patrick Sheehan	1

R

Rory of the Hill	6
Repose: Glengariff	165
Roving Brian O'Connell	260

S

Saint Stephen's Night	4
Success to Eugene	31
Shemus O'Brien	64
Sliav Na Man	147
Spirit Company	173
Shaun's Head	187
Sitting by the Hearth	230
Song of Galloping O'Hogan	233
Song, Not always the Winter	234

T

The Vigil of the Shan Van Vocht	17
Tipperary Recruiting Song	21
The Wearing of the Green	26
To a Furze Bush	38
The Home Rill	41
The Waning of the Year	45
The Irish Peasant Girl	74
The Streams	80
The Gardens of Life	81
The Brothers	92
The Battle of Ardnocher	104
The Young Enthusiast	107
The Boys of Wexford	110

	Page
The Felons	113
The Spinning Wheel	119
The Eviction	121
The Green Little Shamrock	122
The Blarney Stone	124
The Widow's Message	129
The Apostle's Grave	131
The Irish American	134
The Rapparee's Horse and Sword	136
The Fisherman's Prayer	137
The Cailin Deas	139
The New Race	144
The Lullaby	145
The Bard Ethell	154
The Claddagh Boatman	161
The Shan Van Vocht	167
The Shannon	169
The Drinan Donn	171
There are Voices I ween	180
The Sunny South is glowing	192
The Martyr	196
The Irish Mother's Lament	201
The Western Winds	203
The Outlaw's Bridal	213
The Tagus and the Lee	216
The Irish Rapparee	220
The Robin	232
The Little Black Rose	235
The Pass of Plumes	236
The Holly and Ivy Girl	246
The Shamrock	249
The Blacksmith of Limerick	254
The Lupracaun	265
Time's Earthquake	271
The Heather Glenn	272
The Shepherd's Farewell	275
The Clare Election	207
To an Infant: on presenting her with a green top-knot	274

U

Up: written in 1798	268

W

Wishes and Wishes	126

INDEX OF AUTHORS.

A

	Page
ALLINGHAM, WILLIAM.	
Nannie's Sailor Lad	240
Fairies	245
The Lupracaun	265
ANONYMOUS.	
The Vigil of the Shan Van Vocht	17
Tipperary Recruiting Song	21
The Wearing of the Green	26
Our Olden Tongue	29
The Waning of the year	45
Burning of an Emigrant Ship	96
By Memory Inspired	98
Lament of the Ejected Irish Peasant	102
MacKenna's Dream	149
An Caillin Deas	179
There are Voices I ween	180
Music in the Street	181
The Martyr	196
Davis	199
The Western Winds	203
A True Story	209
Up: (written in the year 1798)	209
To an Infant: on presenting her with a green top-knot	274

B

	Page
BRENAN, JOSEPH.	
Dirge for Devin Reilly	9
Florence, my Child	33
Come to me, Dearest	78
An Exile's Dream	116
BROWNE, FRANCES.	
The Streams	80
BOUCICAULT.	
I'm very happy where I am	178

C

	Page
CAMPION, JOHN, M.D.	
The Felons	112
Love in the Country	115
The Outlaw's Bridal	218

	Page
CHERRY, ANDREW.	
The Green Little Shamrock	123

D

	Page
DE VERE, AUBREY.	
Dirge of Rory O'More	44
The New Race	144
The Bard Ethell	154
Song—Not always the Winter	234
The Little Black Rose	235
DOHENY, MICHAEL.	
A cushla gal mo chree	100
DAVIS, FRANCIS.	
Wishes and Wishes	126
DOWLING, J. J., M.D.	
The Claddagh Boatman	161
DUFFY, CHARLES GAVAN.	
The Irish Rapparees	220
DRENNAN, WILLIAM, M.D.	
A Wail	241

E

	Page
FERGUSON, SAMUEL, M.R.I.A.	
Boatman's Hymn	86
FITZGERALD, JOHN.	
The Blarney Stone	124
The Apostle's Grave	131
FORRESTER, ELLEN.	
The Widow's Message	129
FRAZER, J.	
Brosna's Banks	153
FORREST, G. L.	
Blarney Groves	160

G

	Page
GRIFFIN, GERALD.	
A Portrait	91
Nano Nagle	216
The Shannon	169

H

	Page
HOGAN, M.	
Drahareen O Machree	203

L

	Page
IRWIN, THOMAS.	
A Picture of Munster	87
Spirit Company	173
Time's Earthquake	271
The Robin	232
My Violon	239
An Irish Mother's Dream	261

J. Page	Page
JOYCE, ROBERT DWYER, M.D.	Mo Cailin Donn .. 78
Saint Stephen's Night .. 4	The Cailin Deas .. 139
Oh! Fair shines the Sun	Sliav Na Man .. 147
on Glenarn 77	Caitlin Tirrial .. 198
The Boys of Wexford .. 110	After the Clare Election 207
The Rapparee's Horse	Farewell to Pleasant Erinn 225
and Sword 136	Dirge of Oilfeir Gras .. 242
Fineen the Rover .. 143	Gentle Brideen .. 257
The Drinan Donn .. 171	The Heather Glenn .. 272
The Song of Galloping	The Shepherd's Farewell 275
O'Hogan 233	SIGERSON, H.
The Blacksmith of Lim-	Connor's Revenge .. 48
erick 254	The Gardens of Life .. 81
Roving Brian O'Connell 260	SAVAGE, JOHN.
Over the Morning Dew 269	At Niagara 62
K	Shaun's Head 187
KICKHAM, CHARLES J.	SEGRAVE, MICHAEL.
Patrick Sheehan .. 1	The Eviction 12
Rory of the Hills .. 6	SULLIVAN, TIMOTHY D.
The Irish Peasant Girl .. 74	The Irish American .. 125
The Shan Van Vocht .. 167	The Fisherman's Prayer 137
KEEGAN, J.	Michael Dwyer .. 222
Caoch the Piper .. 23	**T**
The Holly and Ivy Girl 246	TREACY, ELIZBTH. WILLOUGHBY.
L	The Irish Mother's La-
LIVINGSTONE, WILLIAM.	ment 201
Success to Eugene .. 31	**V**
LEFANU.	VARIAN, RALPH.
Shemus O'Brien .. 64	Repose: Glengariff .. 165
M	Mo Buachaillin Ban .. 172
MURRAY, FISHER.	Oscar, The Dog of Shaun
To a Furze Bush .. 38	Desmond 185
MACGEOGHEGAN.	He built me a light boat 194
The Battle of Ardnocher 104	Lower Glanmire .. 211
MEAGHER, GENERAL THOMAS	The Tagus and the Lee 216
FRANCIS.	Glendeek 227
The Young Enthusiast 107	Sitting by the Hearth .. 230
M'BURNEY.	The Shamrock .. 249
Arthur MacCoy .. 175	On the Bay 259
MANGAN, CLARENCE.	Mallow 267
Owen Reilly 140	VARIAN, ISAAC S.
Love Ballad 163	Music, music, come, oh!
O	come 109
O'REILLY, PRIVATE MILES.	A Land-Law Rhyme .. 191
April 20th, 1864 .. 20	**W**
O'HERLIHY. PATRICK.	WYLDE, LADY.
A Fragment of M'Au-	The Brothers 92
liffe's Prophecy .. 58	WALLER, JOHN FRANCIS, LL.D.
ORR, ANDREW.	The Spinning Wheel .. 119
The sunny South is glowing 192	WALSH, JOHN.
S	Drimin Donn Dilis .. 132
SIGERSON, GEORGE, M.D.	WALSH, EDWARD.
Irish Lullaby 15	The Lullaby 145
The Home Rill .. 41	WILLIAMS, R. D.
A Snow Song 60	The Pass of Plumes .. 236

POPULAR POETRY
OF IRELAND.

PATRICK SHEEHAN.[*]
Street Ballad.

CHARLES J. KICKHAM.

My name is Patrick Sheehan,
  My years are thirty-four,
Tipperary is my native place,
  Not far from Galtymore;
I came of honest parents—
  But now they're lying low—
And many a pleasant day I spent
  In the Glen of Aherlow.

---

[*] This we found among the street ballad-slips of Dublin and of Cork. On inquiry, we discovered, that it had been written by Charles J. Kickham, of Mullinahone, Co. Tipperary; who, on reading the facts as they were recorded in the newspapers of the day—immediately penned them in the above form of a street ballad, which instantly made its way into the hands of those who cater literature for the illiterate in the form of ha'penny ballads, and became at once a favourite with the people.

My father died; I closed his eyes
  Outside our cabin door—
The landlord and the sheriff too,
  Were there the day before—
And then my loving mother,
  And sisters three also,
Were forced to go with broken hearts
  From the Glen of Aherlow.

For three long months, in search of work,
  I wandered far and near;
I went then to the poor-house
  For to see my mother dear;
The news I heard nigh broke my heart;
  But still, in all my woe,
I blessed the friends who made their graves
  In the Glen of Aherlow.

Bereft of home and kith and kin—
  With plenty all around—
I starved within my cabin,
  And slept upon the ground;
But cruel as my lot was,
  I ne'er did hardship know;
'Till I joined the English army,
  Far away from Aherlow.

" Rouse up there," says the Corporal,
  " You lazy Hirish hound,
Why don't you hear, you sleepy dog,
  The call 'to arms' sound?"

Alas, I had been dreaming
   Of days long, long ago,
I woke before Sebastopol,
   And not in Aherlow.

I groped to find my musket—
   How dark I thought the night;
O blessed God, it was not dark,
   It was the broad daylight!
And when I found that I was *blind*,
   My tears began to flow,
I longed for even a pauper's grave
   In the Glen of Aherlow.

O blessed Virgin Mary,
   Mine is a mournful tale,
A poor blind prisoner here I am,
   In Dublin's dreary jail;
Struck blind within the trenches,
   Where I never feared the foe;
And now I'll never see again
   My own sweet Aherlow!

A poor neglected mendicant
   I wandered through the street,
My nine months' pension now being out,
   I beg from all I meet:
As I joined my country's tyrants,
   My face I'll never show
Among the kind old neighbours,
   In the Glen of Aherlow.

Then Irish youths—dear countrymen—
  Take heed of what I say,
For if you join the English ranks
  You'll surely rue the day;
And whenever you are tempted
  A soldiering to go,
Remember poor blind Sheehan
  Of the Glen of Aherlow.

ST. STEPHEN'S NIGHT.

Robert Dwyer Joyce.[*]

Air—"The Basket of Oysters."

Without, the wild winds keenly blow,
O'er dreary wastes of wintry snow—
Within, the red fire sheds its glow
Where round and round the dancers go!
  Merrily, merrily round and round,
  Airily, airily round and round,
  To the sweetest music in Ireland's ground,
  The heart's glad laugh and the bagpipe's sound!

---

[*] Author of "Ballads, Romances, and Songs," published by James Duffy, Dublin. A native of the County Limerick, from Gleann Oisin.

What befits Saint Stephen's Night,
But loving words and glances bright,
But young and old with main and might,
To dance around in wild delight?
   Merrily, merrily round and round,
   Airily, airily round and round,
   To the sweetest music in Ireland's ground,
   The heart's glad laugh and the bagpipe's sound.

The wren was hunted all the day
By the striplings tall and the children gay;
Now he's dressed in state on the holly spray,
And his noisy captors—where are they?
   Dancing, dancing round and round,
   Airily, airily round and round
   To the sweetest music in Ireland's ground,
   The heart's glad laugh and the bagpipe's sound.

Maid and matron, son and sire,
With bounding spirits that cannot tire,
Around the bright Saint Stephen's fire,
Joke and dance to their hearts' desire,
   Merrily, merrily round and round,
   Airily, airily round and round,
   To the sweetest music in Ireland's ground,
   The heart's glad laugh and the bagpipe's sound.

Round and round so merrily,
But merrier yet that dance would be,
If our scattered brothers beyond the sea
Were home returned, and Ireland free!
   Oh! merrier then we'd dance it round,
   Saint Stephen's Night, around and round,
   To the sweetest music in Ireland's ground,
   The heart's glad laugh and the bagpipe's sound!

RORY OF THE HILLS.

Charles J. Kickham.

"That rake up near the rafters,
   Why leave it there so long?
The handle, of the best of ash,
   Is smooth, and straight, and strong ,
And mother, will you tell me,
   Why did my father frown,
When to make the hay in summer-time,
   I climbed to take it down?"
She looked into her husband's eyes,
   While her own with light did fill,
"You'll shortly know the reason, boy!"
   Said Rory of the Hill.

The midnight moon is lighting up
   The slopes of Sliav-na-man,—
Whose foot affrights the startled hares
   So long before the dawn?
He stopped just where the Anner's stream
   Winds up the woods anear,
Then whistled low and looked around
   To see the coast was clear.
A sheeling door flew open—
   In he stepped with right good will—
"God save all here, and bless your WORK,"
   Said Rory of the Hill.

Right hearty was the welcome
   That greeted him I ween,
For years gone by he fully proved
   How well he loved the Green;

And there was one amongst them
    Who grasped him by the hand—
One who through all that weary time
    Roamed on a foreign strand—
He brought them news from gallant friends
    That made their heart-strings thrill;
"My *sowl !* I never doubted them !"
    Said Rory of the Hill.

They sat around the humble board
    Till dawning of the day,
And yet not song nor shout I heard—
    No revellers were they:
Some brows flushed red with gladness,
    While some were grimly pale;
But pale or red, from out those eyes,
    Flashed souls that never quail !
"And sing us now about the vow,
    They swore for to fulfil"—
"Ye'll read it yet in History,"
    Said Rory of the Hill.

Next day the ashen handle,
    He took down from where it hung.
The toothed rake, full scornfully,
    Into the fire he flung,
And in its stead a shining blade
    Is gleaming once again,
(Oh ! for a hundred thousand of
    Such weapons and such men !)
Right soldierly he wielded it,
    And—going through his drill—
"Attention"—"charge"—"front, point"—"advance !"
    Cried Rory of the Hill.

She looked at him with woman's pride,
    With pride and woman's fears;
She flew to him, she clung to him,
    And dried away her tears;
He feels her pulse beat truly,
    While her arms round him twine—
"Now God be praised for your stout heart,
    Brave little wife of mine."
He swung his first-born in the air,
    While joy his heart did fill—
"You'll be a FREEMAN yet, my boy,"
    Said Rory of the Hill.

Oh! knowledge is a wondrous power,
    And stronger than the wind;
And thrones shall fall, and despots bow,
    Before the might of mind;
The poet, and the orator
    The heart of man can sway,
And would to the kind heavens
    That Wolfe Tone were here to-day!
Yet trust me, friends, dear Ireland's strength,
    Her truest strength, is still,
The rough-and-ready roving boys,
    Like Rory of the Hill.

DIRGE FOR DEVIN REILLY.*

Joseph Brenan.†

[" A few days before Devin died," says a friend, " he expressed a wish to be buried on the slope of a green hill, where his feet could feel the dew, and his eyes look up to the stars."

Thomas Davis expressed a similar wish, and it was very characteristic of the two men; for they had a loving sympathy with all the beautiful things of earth, and a brave upward look for everything grand and worship-worthy in God's universe. That wish has suggested the refrain of the following lines:]

"When the day has come, darling, that your
    darling must go
From the scene of his struggles, of his pride and
    his woe,—
Lay him on a hill-side with his feet to the dew,
Where the soul of the verdure is faintly stealing
    through—
On the slope of a hill with his face to the light,
Which glows upon the dawn and glorifies the night;
For the grand old mother nature is mightier than
    death,
The subtle Irish soul of which the beautiful is
    breath;

---

* From the "New York Citizen"—July 1st, 1854.
† Born in Cork. Was in the dawn of his manhood in Forty-eight, when the inspiration of the Irish national movement absorbed his powers. He subsequently settled in the United States, where he became Editor of "The New Orleans Delta," and married a sister of the Irish refugee, and brother poet, John Savage. Died about five years since, 1859.

Which nestles and dreams in the solemn sounding
  trees,
And flings out its locks to the rapture of the
  breeze,—
And 'twill crave for God's wonders, from the
  daisy star close by,
To the golden scroll which sparkles with his scripture in the sky."

God rest you, Devin Reilly, in the place of your
  choice,
Where the blessed dew is falling and the flowers
  have a voice ;
Where the conscious trees are bending in homage
  to the dead,
And the earth is swelling upward, like a pillow for
  your head ;
And his rest will be with you, for the lonely
  seeming grave,
Though a dungeon to the coward, is a palace to
  the brave,—
Though a black Inferno circle, where the recreant
  are bound,
Is a brave Valhalla pleasure-dome where heroes
  are crowned ;
Oh ! God's rest will be with you, in the congress
  of the great,
Who are purified by sorrow, and are victors over Fate ;
Oh ! God's rest will be with you, in the corridors
  of fame,
Which was jubilant with welcome, when Death
  named your name.

Way 'mongst the heroes for another hero soul!
Room for a spirit which has struggled to its goal!
Rise, for in life he was faithful to his faith,
And entered without stain, 'neath the portico of death,
And his fearless deeds around, like attendant angels stand,
Claiming recognition from the noble and the grand;
Claiming to his meed—who from fresh and bounding youth,
To the days of manly trial, was truthful to the truth—
The welcome of the hero, whose foot would not give way,
'Till his trenchant sword was shivered in the fury of the fray;
And brave will be that welcome if the demi-gods above
Can love with a tithe of our humble mortal love!

" Lay me on a hill-side with my feet to the dew,
Where the life of the verdure is faintly stealing through;
On the slope of a hill, with my face to the light
Which glows upon the dawn, and glorifies the night;"
Would it were a hill-side in the land of the Gael,
Where dew falls like tear-drops, and the wind is a wail;
Where the winged superstitions are gleaming through the gloom,
Like a host of frighted Fairies, to beautify the tomb.
On the slope of a hill with your face to the sky
Which clasp you, like a blessing in the days gone by;

When your hopes were as radiant as the stars of
   the night,
And the reaches of the Future throbbed with constellated light.

Have you seen the mighty tempest, in its war-
   cloak of cloud,
When it stalks thro' the midnight, so defiant and
   proud ;
When 'tis shouldering the ocean, 'till the crouching
   waters fly
From the thunder of its voice and the lightning
   of its eye ;
And the waves, in timid multitudes, are rushing to
   the strand,
In a vain appeal for succor from the buffets of its hand?
Then you saw the soul of Reilly when, abroad in
   its might,
It dashed aside, with loathing, all the creatures of
   the night ;
'Till the plumed hosts were humbled, and their
   crests, white no more,
Were soiled with the sand, and strewn upon the shore;
For the volumed swell of thunder was concentred
   in his form,
And his tread was a conquest and his blow was
   like a storm.

Have you seen a weary tempest, when a harbour
   is near,
And its giant breast is heaving from the speed of
   its career ;

How it puts off its terrors, and is timorous and weak,
As it stoops upon the waters, with its cheek to
 their cheek;
As it broods like a lover, over all the quiet place;
Till the dimpling smiles of pleasure are eddying in
 its trace?
Then you saw the soul of Reilly when ceasing to
 roam,
It flung away the clouds, and nestled to its home;
When the heave and swell were ended, and the
 spirit was at rest,
And gentle thoughts like white-winged birds, were
 dreaming on its breast;
And the tremulous sheets of sunset, around its
 couch were rolled,
In voluptuous festooning of purple, lined with gold.

Oh! sorrow on the day when our young apostle
 died,
When the lonely grave was opened for our darling
 and our pride;
When the passion of a people was following the
 dead,
Like a solitary mourner, with a bowed uncovered
 head;
When a Nation's aspirations were stooping o'er
 the dust;
When the golden bowl was broken, and the
 trenchant sword was rust;
When the brave tempestuous Spirit, with an upward wing had passed,
And the love of the wife, was a widow's love at last;

Oh! God rest you, Devin Reilly, in the shadow
   of that love,
And God bless you with his bliss, in the pleasure
   dome above,
Where the Heroes are assembled, and the very
   angels bow
To the glory of Eternity, which glimmers on each
   brow.

" Lay me on a hill-side with my feet to the dew,
Where the life of the verdure is faintly stealing
   through ;
On the slope of a hill, with my face to the light,
Which glows upon the dawn, and glorifies the
   night ;"
Would it were a hill-side in the land of the Gael,
Where the dew falls like tear-drops, and the wind
   is a wail—
Where the winged superstitions are gleaming
   through the gloom,
Like a host of frighted Fairies to beautify the tomb !
On the slope of a hill with your face to the sky
Which clasped you, like a blessing in the days
   gone by ;
When your hopes were as radiant as the stars of
   the night,
And the reaches of the future throbbed with con-
   stellated light.

IRISH LULLABY.*

(From the Irish.)

GEORGE SIGERSON, TRANSLATOR.†

I'll put you, myself, my baby! to slumber,
Not as is done by the clownish number—
A yellow blanket and coarse sheet bringing,
But in golden cradle that's softly swinging—
      To and fro, lulla lo,
      To and fro, my bonnie baby!
      To and fro, lulla lo,
      To and fro, my own sweet baby!

* The Irish is extracted from the "Ancient Music of Ireland," Vol. I. In reference to the air of the above song Dr. Petrie writes:—"I have already directed attention to the stirking affinity observable between them (the lullabies) and the Eastern melodies of the same class, and I would apply the remarks then made to the beautiful nurse-tune which I am now about to present, and which I think bears equally the stamp of a remote antiquity. I would, moreover add, that such affinity with Eastern melody is not confined to the nurse-tunes of Ireland, but that it will be no less found in the ancient funeral *caoines* as well as in the ploughman's tunes, and other airs of occupation—airs, simple, indeed, in construction, but always touching in expression;—and I cannot but consider it as an evidence of the early antiquity of such melodies in Ireland, and as an ethnological fact of much historic interest, and not hitherto sufficiently attended to."—*Ancient Music of Ireland*, Vol. I.

† Born at Holy Hill, Strabane, Tyrone; author of "Poetry of Munster, Second Series"—a volume of translations from the Irish, published by John O'Daly, Dublin.

I'll put you, myself, my baby! to slumber
On sunniest day of the pleasant Summer;
Your golden cradle on smooth lawn laying,
'Neath murmuring boughs that the winds are swaying
  To and fro, lulla lo,
  To and fro, my bonnie baby!
  To and fro, lulla lo,
  To and fro, my own sweet baby!

Slumber, my babe! may the sweet sleep woo you,
And from your slumbers may health come to you!
May all diseases now flee and fear you;
May sickness and sorrow never come near you!
  To and fro, lulla lo,
  To and fro, my bonnie baby!
  To and fro, lulla lo,
  To and fro, my own sweet baby!

Slumber, my babe! may the sweet sleep woo you,
And from your slumbers may health come to you!
May bright dreams come, and come no other,
And I be never a childless mother—
  To and fro, lulla lo,
  To and fro, my bonnie baby!
  To and fro, lulla lo,
  To and fro, my own sweet baby!

THE VIGIL OF THE SHAN VAN VOCHT.

[Written some twenty-three years ago by an intimate friend of THOMAS DAVIS, and one of the earliest writers in the cause of an uncompromising nationality.]

  'Tis a glorious moonlight night,
    Thought the *Shan van Vocht* ;
  'Tis a glorious moonlight night,
    Said the *Shan van Vocht* :
  So 'twere best to take a stroll,
  Where the foaming billows roll,
  In soft murmurs to my soul,
    Said the *Shan van Vocht.*

  So she went down to the shore,
    Did the *Shan van Vocht,*
  And she heard the billows roar,
    Did the *Shan van Vocht* ;
  And she thought upon the time,
  When in youth's so glorious prime,
  All nature seemed sublime
    To the *Shan van Vocht.*

  Oh! who was once so fair
    As the *Shan van Vocht ?*
  So blithe and free from care,
    As the *Shan van Vocht ?*
  How glorious was her youth!
  How grand her love and truth
  The bitterer now the ruth
    Of the *Shan van Vocht !*

Oh! fearful grew the form
    Of the *Shan van Vocht!*
Like a transfigured storm
    Stood the *Shan van Vocht!*
While the intermingled tide
Of agony and pride,
With pangs intensified,
    Thrilled the *Shan van Vocht!*

For like a tongue of flame,
    To the *Shan van Vocht,*
Was the vision of her shame
    To the *Shan van Vocht!*
Like a fierce avenging flame,
Embracing all her frame,
Was the vision of her shame
    To the *Shan van Vocht!*

The sad sea carolled wild
    To the *Shan van Vocht!*
And the west wind breathed all mild
    On the *Shan van Vocht!*
The waves they sang their psalm,
The west wind brought its balm;
But nought the grief could calm
    Of the *Shan van Vocht!*

And thus the long live night
    Grieved the *Shan van Vocht,*
While moon and sea shone bright
    On the *Shan van Vocht;*

Till at length, at break of day,
She knelt her down to pray,
Then homeward took her way,
    Did the *Shan van Vocht.*

What thoughts the dawn awoke
    In the *Shan van Vocht,*
As the sunrise slowly broke
    On the *Shan van Vocht ;*
Whether terror and despair
Fled from the morning air,
And hope was new-born there,
    For the *Shan van Vocht—*

None know. Still sad and dumb
    Is the *Shan van Vocht,*
But 'tis thought a time will come
    When the *Shan van Vocht,*
New ramparted with truth,
New glorified with youth,
No more can be, in sooth,
    Called the *Shan van Vocht !*

APRIL 20, 1864.
PRIVATE MILES O'REILLY.*

Three years ago to-day
  We raised our hands to Heaven,
And on the rolls of muster
  Our names were thirty-seven;
There were just a thousand bayonets,
  And the swords were thirty-seven,
And we took the oath of service
  With our right hands raised to Heaven.

Oh 'twas a gallant day,
  In memory still adored,
That day of our sun-bright nuptials
  With the musket and the sword!
Shrill rang the fifes, the bugles blared,
  And beneath a cloudless Heaven
Twinkled a thousand bayonets,
  And the swords were thirty-seven.

Of the thousand stalwart bayonets
  Two hundred marched to-day!
Hundreds lie in Virginia swamps,
  And hundreds in Maryland clay;
And other hundreds, less happy, drag
  Their shattered limbs around,
And envy the deep, long, blessed sleep
  Of the battle-field's holy ground.

* Lieut.-Col. C. G. Halpine (born in Dublin) of the famous Irish-American "69th" Regiment.

For the swords—one night, a week ago,
    The remnant just eleven,
Gathered around a banqueting board
    With seats for thirty-seven.
There were two limped in on crutches,
    And two had each but a hand
To pour the wine and raise the cup,
    As we toasted " Our flag and land."

And the room seemed filled with whispers
    As we looked at the vacant seats,
And, with choking throats, we pushed aside
    The rich but untasted meats;
Then in silence we brimmed our glasses,
    As we rose up—just eleven,
And bowed as we drank to the loved and the dead
    Who had made us THIRTY-SEVEN!

TIPPERARY RECRUITING SONG,
STREET BALLAD.

'Tis now we'd want to be wary, boys,
The recruiters are out in Tipperary, boys;
If they offer a glass, we'll wink as we pass—
We're ould birds for chaff in Tipperary, boys.

Then hurrah for the gallant Tipperary boys,
Although we're " cross and contrairy," boys,
The never a one will handle a gun;
Except for the Green and Tipperary, boys.

Now mind what John Bull did here, my boys
In the days of our famine and fear, my boys:
He burned and sacked, he plundered and racked,
Ould Ireland of Irish to clear, my boys.

Now Bull wants to pillage and rob, my boys,
And put the procceds in his fob, my boys;
But let each Irish blade just stick to his trade,
And let Bull do his own dirty job, my boys.

So never to 'list be in haste, my boys,
Or a glass of drugged whiskey to taste, my boys;
If to India you'll go, 'tis to grief and to woe,
And to rot and to die like a beast, my boys.

But now he is beat for men, my boys,
His army is getting so thin, my boys,
With the fever and ague, the sword and the plague,
Oh! the devil a fear that he'll win, my boys.

Then mind not the robbing ould schemer, boys,
Tho' he says that he's richer than Damer, boys;
Tho' he bully and roar, his power is o'er,
And his black heart will shortly be tamer, boys.

Now isn't Bull peaceful and civil, boys,
In his mortal distress and his evil, boys?
But we'll cock each caubeen when his serjeants
    are seen,
And we'll tell them to go to the devil, boys.

Then hurrah for the gallant Tipperary boys!
Altho' we're cross and contrairy, boys,
The never a one will handle a gun,
Except for the Green and Tipperary, boys.

CAOCH* THE PIPER.
J. KEEGAN.†

One winter's day, long, long, ago,
   When I was a little fellow,
A piper wandered to our door,
   Grey-headed, blind, and yellow—
And, oh! how glad was my young heart,
   Though earth and sky looked dreary—
To see the stranger and his dog—
   Poor "Pinch" and Caoch O'Leary.

And when he stowed away his "bag,"
   Crossed-barred with green and yellow,
I thought and said, "In Ireland's ground,
   There's not so fine a fellow."
And Fineen Burke, and Shaun Magee,
   And Eily, Kate, and Mary,
Rushed in, with panting haste to "see,"
   And "welcome" Caoch O'Leary.

Oh! God be with those happy times!
   Oh! God be with my childhood!
When I, bare-headed, roamed all day,
   Bird-nesting in the wild-wood—
I'll not forget those sunny hours,
   However years may vary;
I'll not forget my early friends,
   Nor honest Caoch O'Leary.

* Pronounced Kay-uch, meaning "The Blind."
† Born of humble parents, in the Queen's County, in a village by the Nore, died in 1849, about forty years of age.

Poor Caoch, and "Pinch," slept well that night,
    And in the morning early,
He called me up to hear him play
    "The wind that shakes the barley,"
And then he stroked my flaxen hair,
    And cried—"God mark my deary,"
And how I wept when he said "farewell,
    And think of Caoch O'Leary."

Well—twenty summers had gone past,
    And June's red sun was sinking,
When I, a man, sat by my door,
    Of twenty sad things thinking:
A little dog came up the way,
    His gait was slow and weary,
And at his tail a lame man limped—
    'Twas "Pinch" and Caoch O'Leary!

Old Caoch, but oh! how woe begone!
    His form is bowed and bending,
His fleshless hands are stiff and wan,
    Ay—Time is even blending
The colours on his thread-bare "bag"—
    And "Pinch" is twice as hairy,
And "thin-spare" as when first I saw
    Himself and Caoch O'Leary.

"God's blessing here" the wanderer cried,
    "Far, far, be hell's black viper;
Does any body hereabouts,
    Remember Caoch the Piper?"

With swelling heart I grasped his hand;
   The old man murmured " deary,
Are you the silky-headed child,
   That loved poor Caoch O'Leary ?"

" Yes, yes," I said—the wanderer wept
   As if his heart was breaking—
" And where, *a vic machree*," * he sobbed,
   " Is all the merry-making
I found here twenty years ago ?"—
   "My tale," I sighed, " might weary,
Enough to say—there's none but me
   To welcome Caoch O'Leary."

" Vo, vo, vo!" the old man cried,
   And wrung his hands in sorrow,
" Pray let me in *astore machree*,
   And I'll *go home* to-morrow.
My 'peace is made'—I'll calmly leave
   This world so cold and dreary,
And you shall keep my pipes and dog,
   And pray for Caoch O'Leary."

With " Pinch" I watched his bed that night;
   Next day his wish was granted;
He died—and Father James was brought,
   And the Requiem Mass was chanted.—
The neighbours came;—we dug his grave,
   Near Eily, Kate, and Mary,
And there he sleeps his last sweet sleep—
   God rest you! Caoch O'Leary.

* Son of my heart.

THE WEARING OF THE GREEN.
A STREET BALLAD.—1798.*

I'm a lad that's forced an exile
  From my own native land,
For an oath that's passed against me
  In this country I can't stand;
But while I'm at my liberty
  I will make my escape.
I'm a poor distresséd croppy
  For the Green on my cape!
      For the Green on my cape!
      For the Green on my cape!
I'm distressed—but not dishearten'd—
  For the Green on my cape!

But I'll go down to Belfast
  To see that seaport gay,
And tell my aged parents
  In this country I can't stay,
O 'tis dark will be their sorrow—
  But no truer hearts I've seen,
And they'd rather see me dying
  Than a traitor to the Green!
      O, the wearing the Green!
      O, the wearing the Green!
May the curse of Cromwell darken
  Each traitor to the Green!

* * * * *

* The copy we print from comes to us from the county which held out longest against English invasion—Tyrone, and from one of its towns—Dungannon, which was well known to the Volunteers.

When I went down to Belfast,
　　And saw that seaport grand,
My aged parents blessed me,
　　And blessed poor Ireland.
Then I went unto a captain
　　And bargained with him cheap—
He told me that his whole ship's crew
　　Wore Green on the cape!
　　　　O, the Green on the cape!
　　　　O, the Green on the cape!
God's blessing guard the noble boys
　　With Green on the cape!

'Twas early the next morning
　　Our gallant ship set sail,
Kind Heaven did protect her,
　　With a pleasant Irish gale.
We landed safe in Paris,
　　Where victualling was cheap—
They knew we were United,
　　We wore Green on the cape!
　　　　We wore Green on the cape!
　　　　We wore Green on the cape!
They treated us like brothers
　　For the Green on the cape!

Then forward stepped young Boney,
　　And took me by the hand,
Saying—" How is old Ireland,
　　And how does she stand?"*

* One of the French Generals, who was standing by, when a few years since, a sword was being pre-

"It's as poor, distressed a nation
  As ever you have seen,
They are hanging men and women
  For the wearing of the Green!"
      For the wearing the Green!
      For the wearing the Green!
They are hanging men, and women, too,
  For wearing of the Green!"

"Take courage, now, my brave boys,
  For here you have good frien's,
And we'll send a convoy with you,
  Down by their Orange dens;
And if they should oppose us.
  With our weapons sharp and keen,
We'll make them rue and curse the day
  That e'er they saw the Green!
      That e'er they saw the Green!
      That e'er they saw the Green!
We'll show them our authority
  For wearing of the Green!"

O may the wind of Freedom
  Soon send young Boney o'er,
And we'll plant the Tree of Liberty
  Upon our Shamrock shore;

sented from the Irish people, to Marshal M'Mahon, suddenly turned to John Mitchel, one of the Deputatoin, and addressed him in the very words of this ninety-eight ballad—"How is old Ireland and how does she stand?"

O, we'll plant it with our weapons
 While the English tyrants gape
To see their bloody flag torn down,
 To Green on the cape!
  O, the wearing the Green!
  O, the wearing the Green!
God grant us soon to see that day,
 And freely wear the Green!

OUR OLDEN TONGUE.

ANONYMOUS.

From dim tradition's far-off opal fountains,
 Where clouds and shadows loom;
Deep in the silence of the tall grey mountain's
 Primeval gloom;
Thy silvery stream flows down with music bounding,
 O ancient tongue!
With love, and tears, and laughter softly sounding,
 As wild bird's liquid song.

From winds and waters in their choral mingling,
 Thy honied words were born;   [tingling,
From that strong pulse through Nature's bosom
 In Earth's first morn,
The quivering boughs in forests green and olden,
 With murmurs low,
Rang out such accents beautiful and golden,
 Beneath the dawn's white glow.

Around in mighty characters unfolded,
    The fame we yet discern;
The ivied shrine in grace and grandeur moulded,
    The *cromlec* stern—
The tall slim tower of aspect weird and hoary,
    With dream and *rann*,
Full-crested in its lone and silent glory,
    Fronting the naked sun!

Thou bring'st bright visions—bardic strains enchanting,
    Attuned in lordly halls;
The clash of spears—the banners gaily planting
    On palace walls—
White-bearded sages—warrior-chiefs victorious,
    A goodly throng!
In panoramic pomp of ages glorious,
    Before us pass along.

O'er wide blue plains we see the red deer bounding,
    In flickering shade and sun;
And on this track with deep-toned lay resounding,
    The wolf-hound dun—
Old mountains dim, dark forest, rock and river,
    Those days are o'er;
But shades and echoes people ye for ever,
    And shall till time is o'er!

O! tongue of all our greatness—all our sorrow,
    Shalt thou then fail and fade?
And leave the full hearts mute that ne'er can borrow
    From stranger aid,

Fit utterance for those thoughts whose stormy
    clangour,
        Swells deep within—
The memories of our love, and hate and anger,
    Which nought from us can win ?

Not so—thou hast not stemmed the floods of ages,
    Nor braved a conqueror's sway ;
Thou hast not writ upon the world's wide pages,
    To pass away—
Deep, deep, thy root where never human power,
    May reach to spoil ;
And soon in wealth of vernal leaf and flower,
    Thou'lt deck this olden soil !

SUCCESS TO EUGENE.*

WILLIAM LIVINGSTONE.†

Although for more than twenty years my muse
Has slumbered in the dust ;
Your learning, your repute, your
Wide-spread fame aroused it
    To sing success to Eugene !

* Eugene O'Curry—the late distinguished professor of Irish in the Catholic University of Dublin.
† William Livingstone, of Glasgow. He wrote this address to Eugene O'Curry in the Celtic—the above is a translation.

No longer bound by galling chains,
Green Erinn! lift thy head;
Thy matchless speech impart to all
Thy sons who will proclaim thy fame,
  And the success of Eugene!

The venerable tongue of the Milesian race,
Which always was, and must not fail,
No malice can suppress,
While in the hands and guarded
  With such success by Eugene!

'Tis not the fiery cross, nor other sign of battle,
'Tis not the din of death in pride of the sword;
But the linguial light of the heroes
Who sleep in Inisfail.
  Success to Eugene!

This elegant and many-powered speech,
Whose influence wide Europe owned,
You will replace above all others,
As the very key of knowledge.
  Success to Eugene!

To the land of mountain and flood you are dear;
Old hardy Albyn, with her ancient honours,
Greets you with wide-spread arms,
Despite who would forbid it; and bids
  Success to Eugene!

In the free affection of their Celtic blood,
The plaided heroes here salute you;
With sound of pipe and harmony of harp,
Across the briny deep they shout
  Success to Eugene!

They delight in Erinn's story
Of the hoary ages past;
And as the scribe records it,
They'll joyfully peruse it,
    And chime, success to Eugene!

Show them the wisdom of the worthies,
Oliol, Olamh, and Conall Cearnach;
Shew them Cuchulin in his splendid chariot,
Brian the brave, and others whom you know,
    Success to Eugene!

All here desire your welfare,
Wish you blessing, and honour in every place;
And shall not I also sing,
Joy of my heart, king of the Gaelic,
    Success to Eugene!

FLORENCE, MY CHILD.
Joseph Brennan.

I.

The little footsteps pattering near,
  The little treble voice,
Strike to my soul a sense of fear,
  When I would fain rejoice.

The pretty smile—the ringing laugh—
  The peachy cheek to mine,
The lips whose little kiss I quaff,
  More eagerly than wine.

The childish griefs which quickly crowd
   Behind some wilful deed —
The shadows of a summer cloud
   Upon a summer mead ;

The wayward ways—the baby talk—
   The sudden searching glance,
The gallant strivings made to walk,
   And checked by every chance;

All bring a sense of grief and joy,
   Of blessing and of ban,
Because I see myself a boy,
   And what I am, a man.

Wide are the future's gates unrolled,
   And visions sad and proud;
Come forth—some clad in robes of gold,
   Some shrouded with a shroud.

A host of hopes come forth with them,
   And then a host of fears—
For tho' I see the diadem,
   I see the victor's tears.

And when the night begins to fall,
   I muse with brain o'er-wrought,
Until the shadows on the wall
   Seem mockeries of thought.

II.

In those dark eyes a genius lies,
   A Glory and a Might;
As sleeps within the evening skies
   The coming morning's light.

I recognise the power sublime—
　　The synonym of fame—
Which on the granite walls of Time
　　Cuts deep a deathless name.

I note the glorious strength concealed,
　　Which signalizes life,
The will to clutch and skill to wield
　　A weapon in the strife.

Those little hands, like lily leaves,
　　Are white and frail to view—
But, oh! what work a hand achieves,
　　If but the heart be true!

May not its wondrous labor fill
　　The temple and the mart,
With symbols of its thought and skill
　　And miracles of art?

My child, that forehead pale and wide
　　Contains a busy brain—
Oh! may it know the thinker's pride,
　　But not the thinker's pain!

III.

Red blood is in the veins, my child—
　　The blood of Desmond's race—
Which comes thro' ages undefiled
　　To tingle in thy face.

The blood which never could endure
  To give or take a wrong—
Which paled with pity to the poor,
  And flushed against the strong.

What use? . The bounding blood of yore
  Which thrilled the true and bold,
Is puddle now—for every door
  Is barred with bars of gold.

The clinking of the silver dimes
  Life's melody has marred,
And Nature's immemorial chimes
  Are jangled false, and jarred.

The grandeur of the Grecian past
  No more for earth remains—
Athené's laurel withers fast
  Before the "diggor's" gains.

In bitter jest they call *us* Greeks,
  And yet they touch the truth,
For we can speak the word which speaks
  Of Nature's honest youth.

The word of light, the word of power,
  The word of simple faith,
Which shines beyond the fleeting hour,
  And triumphs over death.

IV.

But see, the night begins to fall,
  My brain is over-wrought—
Those witch-like shadows on the wall
  Seem mockeries of thought.

Must thou, my child, must thou go forth
  To swell the city drove,
And pawn for gold or money's worth
  The beauty of thy love?

Must thou, too, shrink with timid hate,
  As mother and as wife,
From him, thy church-appointed mate,
  Who'll give thy children life?

Sooner the shaft of death may glide
  Amid our transports wild,
And strike thee, not as blighted bride,
  But as a happy child!

Sooner my heart should break to-night
  In this dim, solemn room,
And grieve for all thy wasted light
  Within its silent tomb!

The little faltering footsteps near,
  The little treble voice,
Strike to my soul a sense of fear
  When I would fain rejoice.

TO A FURZE BUSH.
JOHN FISHER MURRAY.*

   The delight
Of summer morn—and mellow-breathing night
   Of June   [forth
Be flowers of southern climes. Thou pourest
Thy tropic odours to the inclement North,
   And late and soon,
Thy verdant altar garlanded appears,
Perennial blooming through th' eternal years!

   On the waste
And desolate hill-side is thy dwelling placed;
   There dost thou grow
A beauty and a blessing—round thee hum
The wilding bees—the flute-voiced linnets come
   There to bestow
Their grateful song on thee, whose guarded breast
Bravely defends their callow fledglings' nest!

   Not thy bloom
Delights me only—not thy rich perfume;
   I love thee more
For thy unchanging verdurous constancy
That great oaks want, and many a summer tree
   When summer's o'er.
So deep a shade, such floods of blossoming light—
Thou art at once bright noon, and mirk midnight!

---

* Author of the "Lines to the memory of Thomas Davis," prefixed to the volume of Davis' poems:—of the ballad "Dark Margaret" (Hayes' Collection) and the "Lost Wife" (Duffy's). A native of Belfast.

Why, Goldsmith, why,
Dost stigmatize in unforgotten lay
"The blossomed furze, *unprofitably* gay?"
Well dost thou know
How profitable beauty is, how bright
The innocent blossom, gladdening our sight
With sun-lit glow.
Dear native Bard, and memorable long,
While there is faith in nature, and in song!

No marvel he,*
Nature's interpreter, beholding thee
With reverence knelt
Before thy incense-bearing altar, there
Adoring HIM who made a thing so fair
As to be felt
By one who SCANIA's bloomless hill-sides trod,
Th' oppressive beauty of the present GOD!

Robust and free,
As best befits the moorland-nurtured child;
Yet pining not in sheltering clime and mild,
If destiny
Hath in the pleasant places cast thy lines;
So the brave soul in every aspect shines,
And blooms as sure
In valley warm and rich, on hill-side cold and poor.

See, it crests
The rifted rocks, and climbs their shaggy breasts,
Like childhood clambering up the knees of age.
The cold grey stone,

* Linnæus, who, coming to these countries and beholding furze for the first time, knelt before it.

With cloth of gold skirting its coat of frieze,
   Dazzles our eyes.
Is not strange such beauty and such bloom,
Out of the heart of cold grey stone could come!

   Dim are mine eyes!
Tear-bringing fancies, home-bred memories,
   Rise, every one,
As from the grave, when I behold thy flowers,
Then I remember me of boyish hours
   And play-mates gone;
Through the long waste of years again I hear
Far up the furzy field their voices loud and clear.

   Ever it clings
Around my heart in joy and sorrow too,
Desire of home, fountain of good and true—
The last abiding joy of all I ever knew.
Dear native shades, and simple people there,
   Whose free hearts share
The plenteous board the liberal hand affords,
And welcomings that have no need of words.

   Beloved spot!
Dwell in my heart, an Eden unforgot.
   In thee were seen
Flowers ever fair, and pastures ever green,
A world to me wert thou the world hath never been,
   Never can be.
There comely maids, there decent matrons came,
And generous youths unknown to vulgar fame.

    I would that one,
For charity, when that my days are done,
Thy seeds might scatter o'er this mouldering breast,
Lending a lustre to my place of rest.
So shall these bones, when life's poor play is o'er,
Borrow in death a grace unknown before ;
        "And like the actions of the just,
         Smell sweet, and blossom in the dust."

THE HOME RILL.
George Sigerson.

Welcome, O little Rill !
    Bright be thou ever,
Green be thy border still,
    Twinkling thy quiver.
Thee I can never pass,
    All unrejoiceful,
Where, through the meadow grass,
    Making it voiceful,
Thou comest, by thyself, dancing and dimpling ;
    Down by the meadow's edge,
    Domed by the drooping sedge,
    Over a lichened ledge,
    Under a whisp'ring hedge,
        Winding and wimpling !

Where, through the little arch,
    Mossy and olden,
Close by a taper larch,
    Under a golden

Bough of sweet-scenting furze,
  Softly outflowing,
Out in clear amber stirs
  Pulsing and glowing,
Thou comest, by thyself, from the mead welling ;
  Out on the dusty way,
  Edging its margin grey,
  With a green broidery,
  And a low melody
    Liquidly knelling !

There, in the mossy brink,
  Warding thy entry,
Sits a wee white and pink
  Daisy-bud sentry.
There, in a shady nook,
  Sunned by their lustre,
Laugh on thee, little brook,
  Laugh in a cluster,
Primroses splendor-ful, radiant and yellow ;
  While in the linden grove,
  Cooeth the brooding dove,
  While from the sky above,
  Show'reth a shower of love,
    Tinklingly mellow !

Years ago—years ago—
  Far in the old days,
When things on high and low
  Beamed through a gold haze,
Thee, as a child, I met—
  Large-eyed in wonder—
Traced thee with small feet wet,
  Up hill and under,

Lured by thy peaceful voice, child-like and lonely.
    Nay, I can pass thee not,
    Memories haunt the spot,
    Shadows come, long forgot,
    Shades of Some who are not,
      Come, alas, only!

    Still grows the iris here,
      Shall I not take one?
    Leaf-shallops launcht we here,
      Shall I not make one?
    Float away, plaited prow,
      'Mong the cress islets,
    Now in mid-stream, and now
      Coasting the violets,
Gone are the wee hands that claspt mine to guide thee,
    Gone the sweet silver shout—
    Gone the laugh ringing out—
    Gone the half-smiling pout—
    Gone all the merry rout
      Running beside thee.

    In my heart, lonely brook,
      Yearns a vague sadness;
    Can'st not one little nook
      Fill with old gladness?
    Whilst the chill grass that forms
      Thy floating fringes,
    Thrilled by thy ripple warms,
      Into rose tinges.
Share me, lone wanderer, share me thy quiet.
    O'er thee the bough that bore
    Snows but a month before,

Buds in green stars all o'er,
Shakes to its gladdened core
  With the birds' riot.

Whisp'ring thyself unto,
  Peaceful communings,
Through my soul gently, too,
  Flow thy sweet croonings.
Fare thee well, little Rill!
  Singing through even,
While other sounds grow still
  'Neath the starred heaven,
Thou goest, by thyself, all thy tones blending,
  Far by the dusty way—
  Far in the farness grey,
  In a soft harmony,
  And a low melody,
    Till the last ending.

DIRGE OF RORY O'MORE.
A.D. 1642.
AUBREY DE VERE.*

Up the sea-saddened valley at evening's decline,
A heifer walks lowing—"the silk of the kine;"†
From the deep to the mountains she roams, and again
From the mountain's green urn to the purple-
    rimmed main.

* Of Curragh Chase, Adare, Co. Limerick; author of some prose works, several volumes of classical and devotional poetry of high repute, and more recently of an excellent volume of poems illustrative of Irish history and character. Genius seems hereditary in his family, as his father, Sir S. de Vere, acquired a distinguished name in the world of letters.
† One of the mystical names of Ireland.

What seek'st thou, sad mother? Thine own is
    not thine!   [brine!
He dropped from the headland—he sank in the
'Twas a dream!—but in dreams at thy foot did
    he follow   [mallow!
Through the meadow-sweet on by the marish and

Was he thine? Have they slain him? Thou
    seek'st him not knowing   [lowing!
Thyself, too, art theirs—thy sweet breath and sad
Thy gold horn is theirs; thy dark eye and thy silk,
And that which torments thee, thy milk is their
    milk!

'Twas no dream, Mother Land! 'Twas no dream,
    Innisfail!   [the Gael!
Hope dreams, but grief dreams not—the grief of
From Leix and Ikerren to Donegal's shore,
Rolls the dirge of thy last and thy bravest—O'More!

THE WANING OF THE YEAR.
Anonymous.

The mist was lifting silver grey
  From off the mountain peaks,
And broke the wild November day
  Behind the purple Reeks;
Upon the lone and stormy glens,
  On Carran-Tual's crown;
And the splinter'd peaks whence rushing Flesk,
  To Lough Lene thunders down,—

When I parted in the gloomy pass,
  With all my heart held dear,
My own lost love and native land,
  In the waning of the year.
The waves went lashing madly up
  The dark lake's stormy marge,
As the wild wind curled the crested foam
  Around my lady's barge.
Her oarsmen bent them to the stroke;
  She sat in dauntless calm,
Her white face raised to the angry heaven,
  The rudder 'neath her palm.
    With a hopeless and a desperate glance,
      That left no place for fear,
    She came to meet her outlaw'd love
      In the waning of the year.

I watched her near the foeman's fort—
  I saw the shot fly fast,—
I marked her look of woman scorn,
  As the slight skiff sped past.
And as the coward Dutchman raised
  The matchlock in his hand,
She kissed the white rose, and she cried—
  "King James and Ireland!"
    For true to king, and land, and faith,
      Was she, my lady dear,
    As her kin who sailed from Limerick town,
      In the waning of the year!

Red gleam'd the flash—the echo rang,
  The light smoke clear'd away—
The hooker's bows came plunging on
  Thro' blinding mist and spray;

And a wild weird shriek rose piercingly
  O'er whistling wind and rain,—
I never heard it's like before,
  And never shall again.
    For the wailer of the princely line
      Of her, my lady dear,
    Sent up her keen with the blast that mourn'd,
      The waning of the year.

There was blood upon her heaving breast
  As they laid her down to die,
And thus to part for aye, we met,
  My promised Bride and I!
We met for such a moment's space!—
  There was so much to say—
So many words of love and faith,
  Ere yet she passed away.
    And so I watched the livelong day,
      And marked the end draw near;
    And her life ebb fast as the twilight fades,
      At the waning of the year!

It came that night! her dying lips
  Pressed to the Cross, her hand
Clasped fast in mine; her latest prayer
  For King and Fatherland—
And for the faith it's noblest held,
  And the bright swords they bore,
All lost, save honour, creed and name,
  To many an alien shore,
    And so she passed to rest in Christ,
      My faithful one and dear,
    The eve we kept our bloody tryste,
      In the waning of the year.

We bore her dust at the dead of night
   Across the wintry hills,
And the torchlight red on the white snow fell
   And on the flashing rills.
Its murky glare lit up the bier
   Where the dead lay fair and cold,
With the white rose on her maiden breast,
   And the blood on her mantle's fold.
     And so, in Muckross choir, I laid
       All that my heart held dear
     In holy earth, with her chieftain sires,
       In the waning of the year.

And round that early grave we swore
   An oath too deep for words,
As on her pure and virgin bier
   We laid our thirsty swords.
And from the traitors' burning tower
   That night rose shriek and groan,
As the murderer's soul went up to stand
   Before the Judgment throne.
     And forth to win a soldier's grave
       I went without a tear;
     For my lady's blood was well avenged
       Ere the waning of the year.

CONNOR'S REVENGE.
H. SIGERSON.

I.

Up in the morning early,
   Rose young Connor to his work,
To his daily toil for Agent Lee,
   On the lands of Glenatore;

The morn was bright in bars of gold
  Across his cottage floor,
And rosily the sun shone in
  When he unlatched the door.

And from the wood and heathy hill,
  The gladd'ning airs came in,
Like the coming of his own true love —
  His darling Kathaleen—
'Tis often she was in his thoughts,
  Through morn and night and noon,
For " Connor Og"* was deep in love,
  As you will know full soon.

Beside the door a while he stood,
  And thought upon his dear,
While gazing on the rosy sky,
  That morning bright and clear;
'Twas—" Oh !" he sighed, " I wish—I wish
  She were this day my bride,"
But then he heard his mother moan,
  Lonely and sick inside.

And to her darken'd room he went,
  From his dreams in the dawning bright,
And gently asked her how she was,
  And how she'd spent the night ?
For, ah ! he was a kind young lad,
  His mother's only son,
And a clever, stately, handsome lad,
  As ever sun shone on !

* " Connor Og"—i.e. Young Connor.

He lit the faggots, piled the turf,
  With kind and ready art;
While silently the mother blessed
  The darling of her heart:—
"There, go *astor!* your master's hard,
  And the day is getting late."
"But I must to the well, mother,"
  He said—and thought of Kate.

And so with pitchers twain went he,
  Soft whistling in tune,—
As through the dewy fields he trod,—
  The air of Paistin Fionn,*
And who but she, his fair Paistin,
  Was waiting by the well—
It made his heart beat quick with joy,
  He would not dare to tell.

For though she brought her pitcher there,
  And loitered in the sun,
Her mother had "three cows," *movrone!*
  His mother had not one;
Yet often by the well at morn,
  Or dusky evening late,
There came to tease his very heart,
  The roguish eyes of Kate!

And who could blame her love or his;
  They both were fond and fair,
And if *the cows* would but agree,
  Were suited to a hair;

---

* Paistin Fionn, pronounced in Munster "Paushteen Fiune," signifies a "fair little child," and is used as a term of endearment to fair young women.

No scene of fawning love could paint
    Their modest sly advances,
Besides it had not come to words,
    And who could write the glances!
'Twas but :—" A blithe good morrow, Conn,
    And how is your poor mother ?"
And while they praised the morning bright,
    They smiled upon each other ;
Now round her he must fold the cloak,
    That slipped by some strange miss,
And though " it had not come to words,"
    He finished with a kiss!

" Now, Conn, behave! you'd better go—
    At work you'll sure be late ;"
" *A's truagh!*"—but I'll be home with you—
    One moment—do but wait ;"
She would not wait, yet did not go,
    But with a busy look,
She stood, and bound her tresses fair
    Beside the rippling brook!

II.

The bird that flies to guard her young,
    Could not more eager prove,
Than Connor, when he hurried back,
    Upon the wings of love ;
With glowing cheek, and beaming eyes,
    He hastened to her side,
Yet strove in laugh and jesting words,
    His panting haste to hide.

Through wild borheen, by Kyle's green wood,
    To where the roses grew,
They loitered on in playful mood,
    Till near her gate they drew ;

    * What sorrow!

And there a while they parting stood,
  As lovers will delay,
Until they heard a horse's hoofs,
  Come patt'ring down the way.

'Twas Jonas Kyle, the landlord's son,
  In scarlet trim he went,
To meet a party in the Glenn,
  Who were on hunting bent;
He smiled and kissed his hand to Kate;
  Who blushing smiled again,
But when he saw poor Conn, he frowned,
  And sharply drew the rein.

" Is this your *work*, you worthless boor ?"
  He cried with curling lip,
And whether by design or chance,
  He struck him with his whip;
The young man turned with clenched hand,
  And brow of crimson shame,
But curb'd his wrath with sullen groan,
  And muttering, curs'd his name.

And while he trod the weary road
  That led away from Kate,
His poor young heart was sorely rent
  With anger, love and hate;
For Jonas Kyle was coarse of soul
  And hated by the poor,
For "knavish boors" he curs'd them all,
  But he—he was the boor!

His father's tenants were no more
  Than cattle in his way,
Their only use to toil for him
  And his rack-rents to pay;

But Connor's proud and manly mien
    Did chiefly rouse his hate,
And most of all, when with him smiled,
    The village beauty, Kate.

*   *   *   *   *   *

Loud bay the dogs in Allaglen,
    And hot the huntsmen ride
O'er many a brake and briery fence,
    And up the mountain side,
Until at length they sweep the wood
    And fields of Captain Kyle,
Where Jonas, with a friend or two,
    Turn in to rest awhile.

"Now," swears he, with a brutal oath,
    "What mean these idle hounds?
By —— there's not a man at work
    On all my father's grounds!"
And true it was and strange to see
    The labourers idle stand,
And not a plough or spade or horse
    At work upon the land.

In idle groups they, whisp'ring, stand,
    Or loiter up and down,
Nor answer to his angry threats,
    Save with a gloomy frown;
He enters at the wide park-gate
    And there sees Agent Lee,
And loud to his admiring friends,
    Thus brutally spake he:—

"Ho! here's the master of the men,
　　Half blind, and deaf and grey,
And when the cat is blind and deaf,
　　The mice you see will play;
Yet surely to his master,
　　He is suited well, I own,
But faith they'll play another game
　　When I shall have my own.

"When I shall have my own, by —— !"
　　With harsh loud laugh, he said.
"You have it now, young man," said Lee,
　　"Old Captain Kyle is dead!
Dead in his bed, this morning,
　　Neglected and alone—
While strangers wept to hear him call
　　So vainly for his own."

PART III.

The night was black, and the piercing wind
　　Swept, howling, through Kyle's wood,
And moaning, wept in frozen tears,
　　Round where Conn's home had stood;
But it could not, to the pitying mind,
　　So keen a chill impart,
As the bitter tears and rending sobs
　　Of a woman's breaking heart.

Two women crouched beneath a shed,
　　Beside the ruined cot,
And one with ceaseless anguish wept—
　　The other heard her not;

For in the grasp of death she lay
   On a poor bed of straw,
Her face was white—her eyes were fixed—
   God knows what then she saw.

" My father and my mother,
   They cursed me night and day,
Because, unknown, I left them both,
   And married Conn O'Shea;
And, oh! their curse is heavy now,
   And dark it clings to me—
But I would follow Conn O'Shea,
   Were it to the gallows tree!

" O Connor! *vourneen deelish!*
   While the life is in my heart,
'Till cold in death, from you or yours,
   I'll never, never part;
But may the black curse wither him,
   Who wrought our doleful fate—
The Lord forgive my wicked words,
   My trouble is so great!"

'Twas thus in hoarse and broken sobs
   The poor young girl wept;
While closer to the dying,
   On the scanty straw she crept—
" O, mother dear, the Lord is kind,
   And to your rescue came,
For this good gift of death on earth,
   I bless His holy name.

" But Conn, *astor!* why don't you come?
    She cannot linger on ;
Oh ! come and see your mother once
    Before the life is gone !"
And who was he who watched outside,
    Half naked in the blast,
And from the night such ghastly looks
    Into the hovel cast?

To the loved treasure of his soul,
    He can bring no relief,
And round their hut, all in the dark,
    He hovers like a thief ;
And looks—and looks again—with fear,
    Upon his darling Kate,
And thinks again of Jonas Kyle
    With thoughts of madd'ning hate.

All day no food has passed his lips,
    But he feels not hunger's pain,
For pangs more cruel rend his heart,
    And burn within his brain ;
A dreadful fiend is at his side,
    And bears him company,
And gazes in his pallid face,
    With looks of hellish glee.

And points, and points to the ruin'd wall—
    To something that lies hid—
Something that Connor thrice before
    Had darkly visited ;

And now he draws it slowly forth
   And turns it in his hands—
His brain is reeling round and round—
   He trembles where he stands.

A scorching heat is in his blood,
   Though the piercing wind still blows,
As down the gloomy field he treads,
   Low mutt'ring as he goes;
Low mutt'ring through his clenchéd teeth—
   " I'll watch beside the well—
'Tis but a devil less on earth
   And a devil more in Hell!"

But see the dying woman now—
   She rises stiff and stark,
And with her glazed and hollow eyes
   Is staring through the dark;
"O Holy Virgin!" murmurs Kate,
   And shrinking faints away,
While like a spectre through the night
   Still gazes Anne O'Shea.

At length her numb'd lips find a voice,
   A piteous wail of woe—
"My son—my son—*Fareer, mo leun!**"
   She mutter'd, hoarse and slow,
For she had seen, with knowledge strange,
   And heard, with hearing keen—
Her parting soul, in spirit-life,
   With her dear son had been.

* "Alas! my bleeding anguish."

And her mute breast had felt the storm,
  With which he now did strive;
For love still grappling close with death,
  Had kept her heart alive;
And now she knows he points the gun—
  The flash seems through her brain,
As falls the brutal Jonas Kyle,
  Never to rise again.

A FRAGMENT OF M'AULIFFE'S PROPHECY.

Translated from the Irish.

PATRICK O'HERLIHY.*

O woful are the tidings
  Reveal'd to me this day,
The gen'rous race of Eibhir shall
  Be banish'd far away;
The foe shall come and parcel out
  Their hills and valleys green
Among his serfs:—great changes then
  In Erinn will be seen.

His vassals they shall dwell in
  The brown moors on ev'ry side;
His oxen they shall browse upon
  Your smooth plains far and wide;

---

* Of Muskerry, south of Ireland; lineal descendant of the Eirenachs of St. Gobnate; a Celtic scholar and File.

His herds shall graze in meadows
    The fairest in the land—
I fear me he will leave you nought
    Whereon your homes may stand.

A minion of the stranger
    In each corner shall be seen,
Close watch'd will be the man who dare
    Be partial to The Green;
And if he should prove troublesome—
    In Erinn's cause grown bold—
To him will freely offer'd be
    The cursed Saxon gold.

My heart, alas! is very sad
    At what I must relate;
The haughty Saxon *bodaghs* will
    Expel the Good and Great;
Their poor and suffering clansmen
    They'll banish o'er the sea,
Or drive them to the bleakest cliffs;
    A woeful sight to see!

But sure I am that God will not
    Desert dear Innisfail,
For Freedom yet will raise her head
    Triumphant in Kinsale,
And Cork will send a mighty host,
    Determined, tried, and true,
And Waterford forget that e'er
    This foreign yoke she knew.

Unjust are the incredulous:—
    The men who doubt my lay—

For wrongs avenged this heart of mine
    Will gladden in the clay;
A fierce and bloody battle,
    With sword, and pike, and gun,
From Erinn's shores, in dire dismay,
    Shall make the Saxon run.

O ye, the hoarders up of wealth,
    Unto my tale give ear;
To Mammon your base hearts incline,
    And scanty is your cheer;
Trust me, your ill-got treasure will
    By Saxon hands be wrung
From out of yours—M'Auliffe then
    You'll say has truly sung.

A SNOW SONG.
George Sigerson.

The heathery hills are covered with snow,
The flakes are floating and falling slow,
The tame, wee robin is cheeping low—
    Bare hedges give no cover;
The ice-pond chirps, the cold winds sweep
I pity the poor, little mountain sheep,
So slumber, baby, slumber and sleep
    'Till winter days are over.

The bore-trees creak, the woods deplore,
Long icicles hang, the panes before—
I wonder what sound moves up to the door,
    Or who may be this rover—

Thou shivering snow-child! come to the heat—
I pity all poor, little naked feet
That wander and tremble thro' snow and sleet
    'Till winter days are over.

Now, baby dearie! what think you
To clothe each poor cold foot in a shoe?
You need not crow, for your's will not do
    My merry, little lover!
Your one, lost brother, my baby fair,
His shoes will never and never wear,
They'll be this little one's gladd'ning share
    'Till winter days are over.

For swine are housed, and kine are warm,
The dog by the fireside dreads no harm—
And ah! to see Christ's child in the storm,
    A wanderer without cover.
'Tis sweet to have, but not all to keep,
And 'tis good, sometimes, to know to weep,
And I pity the heart that would slumber and sleep
    'Till winter days are over.

AT NIAGARA.
John Savage.*
The Rapids.

In broken lines, like ghosts of buried nations,
  Struggling beneath their white and tangled palls,
They leap and roar to Earth their exaltations,
  And Earth e'en trembles as the spectre falls.

With strength that gives solemnity to clangour,
  With quaint immensity that strangles mirth,
Like mortal things they roar to time their anger,
  Like things immortal they disdain the Earth.

They bound—as dallying in their gorgeous West,
  In forest cradles and in parent mountains,
They heard old Ocean throb his regal breast
  And call his vassals—the cascades and fountains.

From crag to crag they leap and spread the sound
  Through gorge and wood their flashing banners motion,
Till here in frantic rivalry they bound,
  These mighty white-plumed cohorts, for the ocean.

Surging along the pale battalions muster,
  Crowding each other till the strongest springs
A-top his fellows, with heroic lustre,
  And dares the deeds, like Viking, that he sings.

---

* An Irishman, living in America; brother-in-law of the late Joseph Brenan; a man, himself, of distinguished literary reputation. His tragedy of "Sybil" had a great success on the American stage. And some of his poems have been recited to immense audiences on the platforms of the lecture-halls of the States.

Like men, the Rapids, born 'mid restless valor,
  Flash o'er their foes with many a frothened spasm,
And linking all in pomp's majestic pallor,
  Leap like ten thousand Romans down the chasm!

THE FALLS.

There is an awful eloquence around—
  Like earthquake underneath the dreamful pillows
Of some great town, that deemed its strength profound,
  And wakes on worse than frantic Ocean's billows.

The mists, like shadowy cathedrals, rise,
  And through the vapory cloisters prayers are pouring:
Such as ne'er sprang to the eternal skies
  From old Earth's passionate and proud adoring.

There is a voice of Scripture in the flood,
  With solemn monotone of glory bounding,
Making all else an awe-hushed solitude
  To hear its everlasting faith resounding.

There is a quiet on my heart like death,
  My eyes are gifted with a strange expansion,
As if they closed upon my life's last breath,
  And oped to measure the eternal mansion.

I see so much I fear to trust my vision,
  I hear so much I doubt my mortal ear,
I feel so much, my soul in strong submission
  Bends in a silent, death-like rapture here.

SHEMUS O'BRIEN:

A Tale of 'Ninety-Eight,

As Related by an Irish Peasant.

LEFANU.

Jist after the war, in the year 'Ninety-Eight,
As soon as the Boys wor all scattered and bate,
'Twas the custom, whenever a peasant was got,
To hang him by trial—barrin' such as was shot.

There was trial by jury goin' on by day-light,
And the martial law hangin' the lavings by night.
It's them was hard times for an honest gossoon;
If he missed in the judges he'd meet a dragoon;

An' whether the sojers or judges gave sentence,
The devil a much time they allowed for repentance;
An' the many a fine Boy was then on his keepin',
With small share of restin' or sittin' or sleepin'.

An' because they loved Erinn, and scorned to sell it,
A prey for the bloodhound, a mark for the bullit—
Unsheltered by night and unrested by day,
With the heath for their barrack, revenge for
    their pay.

An' the bravest an' honestest Boy of thim all
Was Shemus O'Brien, from the town of Glingall;
His limbs wor well set, an' his body was light,
An' the keen-fangéd honnd had not teeth half
    as white.

But his face was as pale as the face of the dead,
An' his cheek never warm'd with the blush of
   the red;
An' for all that, he wasn't an ugly young Boy,
For the devil himself couldn't blaze with his eye.

So droll an' so wicked, so dark an' so bright,
Like a fire-flash that crosses the depth of the night;
An' he was the best mower that ever has been,
An' the elegantest hurler that ever was seen:

In fencin' he gave Patrick Mooney a cut,
An' in jumpin' he bate Tom Molony a foot;
For lightness of foot there was not his peer,
For, by Heavens! he almost outrun the red deer;

An' his dancin' was such, that the men used to
   stare,
And the women turn crazy, he did it so quare;
An' sure the whole world gave in to him there!

An' it's he was the Boy that was hard to be caught,
An' it's often he ran, an' it's often he fought,
An' it's many the one can remember right well
The quare things he did, and its oft I heerd tell

How he frighten'd the magistrates, in Cahirbally,
An' escaped through the sojers in Aherloe valley,
An' leather'd the yeomen, himself agen four,
An' stretched the four strongest on old Galtimore.

But the fox must sleep sometimes, the wild deer
   must rest,
And treachery prey on the blood of the best:
D 2

An' many an action of power an' of pride,
An' many a night on the mountain's bleak side,
And a thousand great dangers an' toils overpast,
In darkness of night he was taken at last.

Now Shemus look back on the beautiful moon,
For the door of the prison must close on you soon ;
An' take your last look at her dim misty light,
That falls on the mountain an' valley to-night.

One look at the village, one look at the flood,
An' one at the sheltering far-distant wood :
Farewell to the forest, farewell to the hill,
An' farewell to the friends that will think of you still.

Farewell to the patthern, the hurliu', an' wake,
An' farewell to the girl that would die for your sake !
An' twelve sojers brought him to Maryborough jail,
An' with irons secured him, refusin' all bail.

The fleet limbs wor chained and the sthrong hands wor bound,
An' he lay down his lenth on the cold preson ground,
And the dhrames of his childhood kem over him there,
As gentle and soft as the sweet summer air ;

An' happy rimimbrance crowdin' an ever,
As fast as the foam flakes dhrift down an the river,
Bringin' fresh to his heart merry days long gone by,
Till the tears gathered heavy an' thick in his eye.

But the tears didn't fall, for the pride iv his heart
Wouldn't suffer one dhrop down his pale cheek to start ;
An' he sprang to his feet in the dark preson cave,
An' he swore with a fierceness, that misery gave,

By the hopes iv the good an' the cause iv the brave,
That when he was mouldering in the cowld grave,
His inimies never should have it to boast
His scorn iv their vengeance one moment was lost.
His bosom might bleed, but his cheek should be dhry,
For undaunted he lived, and undaunted he'd die.

PART SECOND.

Well, as soon as a few weeks were over an' gone,
The terrible day of the trial came on ;
There was such a crowd, there was scarce room to stand,
An' sojers on guard, an' dragoons sword in hand.

An' the court-house so full that the people were bother'd,
An' attornies and criers on the point of being smother'd ;
An' counsellors almost gave over for dead,
An' the jury sittin' up in the box over-head.

An' the judge settled out so determined an' big,
An' the gown on his back, an' an elegant wig,
An' silence was call'd, an' the minute 'twas said,
The court was still as the heart of the dead.

An' they heard but the opening of one prison-lock,
An' Shemus O'Brien kem into the dock.—

For one minute he turned his eyes round on the
 throng,
An' then looked on the bars, so firm and so strong.

An' he saw that he had not a hope nor a friend,
A chance to escape, nor a word to defend ;
An' he folded his arms as he stood there alone,
As calm an' as cold as a statue of stone.

An' they read a big writin', a yard long at least,
An' Shemus didn't see it, nor mind it a taste,
An' the judge took a big pinch of snuff, an' he
 says :—
"Are you guilty or not, Jim O'Brien, if you
 please ?"

An' all held their breath in silence of dread,
An' Shemus O'Brien made answer an' said :—
"My lord, if you ask me if in my life-time
I thought any treason, or did any crime,

That should call to my cheek, as I stand alone here,
The hot blush of shame or the coldness of fear,
Though I stood by the grave to receive my death
 blow,
Before God an' the world I would answer you No!

But if you would ask me, as I think it like,
If in the rebellion I carried a pike,
An' fought for ould Ireland, from the first to the
 close,
An' shed the heart's blood of her bitterest foes—

I answer you YES; an' I tell you again,
Though I stand here to perish, it's my glory that
    then
In her cause I was willin' my veins should run dry,
An' that now for her sake I am ready to die."

Then the silence was great, and the jury smiled
    bright,
An' the judge wasn't sorry the job was made light;
By my soul its himself was the crabbed ould chap!
In a twinkling he pulled on his ugly black cap.

Then Shémus's mother, in the crowd standin' by,
Called out to the judge with a pitiful cry,
"Oh! judge, darlin' don't,—oh! don't say the
    word!
The crathur is young—have mercy, my lord!

"You don't know him, my lord; oh! don't give
    him to ruin!
He was foolish—he didn't know what he was doin',
He's the kindliest crathur, the tinderest hearted;—
Don't part us for ever, we that's so long parted!

"Judge mavourneen, forgive him—forgive him,
    my lord!
An' God will forgive you—oh! don't say the
    word!"—
That was the first minute O'Brien was shaken,
When he saw that he was not quite forgot or
    forsaken!

An' down his pale cheek, at the word of his mother,
The big tears were running, one after the other,

An' two or three times he endeavoured to spake,
But the strong manly voice used to falter an'
  break.

But at last, by the strength of his high-mounting
  pride,
He conquer'd an' master'd his grief's swelling tide;
An' says he, "Mother, don't—don't break your
  poor heart,
Sure, sooner or later, the dearest must part.

"An' God knows its better than wand'ring in fear
On the bleak trackless mountain among the wild
  deer,
To be in the grave, where the heart, head, an'
  breast
From labour an' sorrow for ever shall rest.

"Then mother, my darlin', don't cry any more—
Don't make me seem broken in this my last hour;
For I wish, when my heart's lyin' under the raven,
No true man can say that I died like a craven."

Then towards the judge Shemus bent down his
  head,
An' that minute the solemn death-sentence was
  said.

PART THIRD.

The mornin' was bright, an' the mists rose on high,
An' the lark whistled merrily in the clear sky,—
But why are the men standing idle so late?
An' why do the crowd gather fast in the street?

What come they to talk of?—what come they to see?
An' why does the long rope hang from the cross
 tree?
Oh! Shemus O'Brien, pray fervent an' fast,
May the saints take your soul, for this day is your
 last.

Pray fast an' pray strong, for the moment is nigh,
When strong, proud, an' great as you are, you
 must die!—
At last they drew open the big prison gate,
An' out came the Sheriffs an' sojers in state.

An' a cart in the middle, an' Shemus was in it—
Not paler, but prouder than ever, that minit,
An' as soon as the people saw Shémus O'Brien,
Wid prayin' an' blessin', an' all the girls cryin',

A wild wailin' sound kem on all by degrees,
Like the sound of the lonesome wind blowin'
 through trees!
On, on to the gallows the Sheriffs are gone,
An' the car an' the sojers go steadily on.

An' at every side swellin' around of the cart,
A wild sorrowful sound that would open your
 heart.—
Now under the gallows the cart takes its stand,
An' the hangman gets up with a rope in his hand.

An' the priest havin' blest him, gets down on the
 ground,
An' Shemus O'Brien throws one look around.

Then the hangman drew near, and the people grew still,
Young faces turn sickly, an' warm hearts turn chill;

An' the rope bein' ready, his neck was made bare,
For the gripe of the life-strangling cords to prepare;
An' the good priest has left him, havin' said his last prayer.

But the good priest did more—for his hands he unbound,
An' with one daring spring Jim has leap'd on the ground!
Bang! bang! go the carbines, an' clash go the sabres:
He's not down! he's alive! now attend to him, neighbours!

By one shout from the people the heavens are shaken,—
One shout that the dead of the world might awaken;
Your swords they may glitter, your carbines go bang,
But if you want hangin' 'tis yourselves you must hang.

To night he'll be sleepin' in Aherloe glin,
An' the devil in the dice if you catch him agin;
The sojers run this way, the Sheriffs run that,
An' Father Malone lost his new Sunday-hat.

An' the Sheriffs were, both of them, punished
  severely,
An' fined like the devil, because Jim done them
  fairly.

A week after this time, without firin' a cannon,
A sharp Yankee schooner sailed out of the Shannon;
An' the captain left word he was goin' to Cork,
But the devil a bit—he was bound for New York.

The very next spring—a bright mornin' in May,—
An' just six months after the great hangin' day,—
A letter was brought to the town of Kildare,
An' on the outside was written out fair :—

"To ould Mrs. O'Brien, in Ireland, or elsewhere."
An' the inside began—" My Dear good ould Mother,
I'm safe, an' I'm happy—an' not wishin' to bother
You in the radin'—with the help of the priest—
I send you inclosed in this letter, at least,
Enough to pay him an' to fetch you away
To the land of the free an' the brave—Amerikay !
Here you'll be happy, an' never made cryin'
As long as you're mother of Shemus O'Brien.

Give my love to sweet Biddy, an' tell her beware
Of that spalpeen who calls himself 'Lord of Kil-
  dare ;'
An' just say to the judge, I don't now care a rap
For him, or his wig, or his dirty black cap.

An' as for the dragoons—them paid men of
  slaughter—
Say I love them as well, as the devil loves holy water.

An' now, my good mother, one word of advice—
Fill your bag with potatoes, an' bacon, an' rice.

An' tell my sweet Biddy, the best way of all
Is now, an' for ever to leave ould Glengall,
An' come with you, takin' a snug cabin berth,
An' bring us a sod of the ould Shamrock earth.

An' when you start from ould Ireland take passage
   at Cork,
An' come straight across to the town of New York;
An' there ask the Mayor the best way to go
To the town of Cincinnatti—the state Ohio;
An' there you will find me, without much tryin',
At the 'Harp an' the Eagle' kept by Shemus
   O'Brien."

THE IRISH PEASANT GIRL.*

CHARLES J. KICKHAM.

She lived beside the Anner,
  At the foot of Shev-na-mon,
A gentle peasant girl
  With mild eyes like the dawn;
Her lips were dewy rose-buds—
  Her teeth, of pearls rare—
And a snow-drift 'neath a beechen bough
  Her neck and nut-brown hair.

* This little poem when it first appeared in "The Celt" a few years since, was pronounced "a gem" by the late Michael Doheny.

How pleasant 'twas to meet her
  On Sunday, when the bell
Was filling with its mellow tones,
  Lone wood and grassy dell;
And when at eve young maidens
  Strayed the river bank along—
The widow's brown-haired daughter
  Was loveliest of the throng.

O brave, brave Irish girls —
  We well may call you brave!—
Sure the least of all your perils
  Is the stormy ocean wave,
When you leave our quiet valleys,
  And cross the Atlantic's foam—
To hoard your hard-won earnings
  For the helpless ones at home.

"Write word to my own dear mother—
  Say, we'll meet with God above;
And tell my little brothers
  I send them all my love;
May the angels ever guard them,
  Is their dying sister's prayer—"
And folded in the letter
  Was a braid of nut-brown hair.

Ah, cold, and well nigh callous,
  This weary heart has grown
For thy helpless fate, dear Ireland,
  And for sorrows of my own—
Yet a tear my eye will moisten,
  When by Anner side I stray,
For the lily of the mountain foot,
  That wither'd far away.

MO CAILIN DONN.
GEORGE SIGERSON.
(*May*, 1859.)
AIR—" The River Roe," or " Irish Molly O."

The blush is on the flower, and the bloom is on the tree,
And the bonnie, bonnie sweet birds are carolling their glee;
And the dews upon the grass are made diamonds by the sun,
All to deck a path of glory for my own Cáilin Donn!*

   O, fair she is! O, rare she is! O, dearer still to me!
   More welcome than the green leaf to winter-stricken tree,
   More welcome than the blossom to the weary dusty bee,
   Is the coming of my true love—my own Cáilin Donn!

O, Sycamore! O, Sycamore! wave, wave your banners green—
Let all your pennons flutter, O, Beech! before my queen!
Ye fleet and honied breezes, to kiss her hand ye run,
But my heart has passed before ye—to my own Cáilin Donn!

   O, fair she is! &c.

Ring out, ring out, O, Linden! your merry leafy bells!
Unveil your brilliant torches, O, Chestnut! to the dells;

  * *Colleen don*, a " brown (haired) girl."

Strew, strew the glade with splendour, for morn —
  it cometh on!
O, the morn of all delight to me — my own Cáilin
  Donn!

   O, fair she is! &c.

She is coming, where we parted, where she wanders
  every day;
There's a gay surprise before her who thinks me
  far away!
O, like hearing bugles triumph when the fight of
  Freedom's won,
Is the joy around your footsteps — my own Cáilin
  Donn!

 O, fair she is! O, rare she is! O, dearer still to me!
 More welcome than the green leaf to winter-
  stricken tree,
 More welcome than the blossom to the weary
  dusty bee,
 Is your coming, O, my true love — my own
  Cáilin Donn!

OH! FAIR SHINES THE SUN ON GLENARA.

Robert D. Joyce.
Air — "Glenara."

Oh! fair shines the sun on Glenara,
And calm rest his beams on Glenara;
 But oh! there's a light
 Far dearer, more bright,
Illumines my soul in Glenara,
The light of thine eyes in Glenara.

And sweet sings the stream of Glenara,
Glancing down through the woods like an arrow;
    But a sound far more sweet
    Glads my heart when we meet
In the green summer woods of Glenara,—
Thy voice by the wave of Glenara.

And oh! ever thus in Glenara,
Till we sleep in our graves by Glenara,
    May thy voice sound as free
    And as kindly to me,
And thine eyes beam as fond in Glenara,
In the green summer woods of Glenara!

COME TO ME, DEAREST.
Joseph Brenan.[*]

Come to me, dearest, I'm lonely without thee.
Day-time and night-time I'm thinking about thee;
Night-time and day-time in dreams I behold thee,
Unwelcome the waking which ceases to fold thee.
Come to me, darling, my sorrows to lighten,
Come in thy beauty to bless and to brighten,
Come in thy womanhood, meekly and lowly,
Come in thy lovingness, queenly and holy.

Swallows will flit round the desolate ruin,
Telling of Spring and its joyous renewing;
And thoughts of thy love, and its manifold treasure,
Are circling my heart with a promise of pleasure;
O, Spring of my spirit, O, May of my bosom,
Shine out on my soul till it burgeon and blossom—
The waste of my life has a rose root within it,
And thy fondness alone to the sunshine can win it.

[*] Addressed to his wife.

Figures that move like a song through the even—
Features lit up by a reflex of heaven—
Eyes like the skies of poor Erinn, our mother,
Where the shadows and sunshine are chasing each
    other;
Smiles coming seldom, but child-like and simple,
Planting in each rosy cheek a sweet dimple,—
Oh! thanks to the Saviour, that even thy seeming
Is left to the exile to brighten his dreaming!

You have been glad when you knew I was gladdened;
Dear, are you sad now to hear I am saddened?
Our hearts ever answer in tune and in time, love,
As octave to octave and rhyme unto rhyme, love;
I cannot weep but your tears will be flowing—
You cannot smile but my cheeks will be glowing—
I would not die without you at my side, love—
You will not linger when I shall have died, love.

Come to me, dear, ere I die of my sorrow,
Rise on my gloom like the sun of to-morrow,
Strong, swift and fond as the words which I speak,
    love,   [love;
With a song on your lip and a smile on your cheek,
Come, for my heart, in your absence is weary—
Haste, for my spirit is sickened and dreary:
Come to the arms which alone should caress thee;
Come to the heart which is throbbing to press thee.

THE STREAMS.

Frances Brown.*

Your murmurs bring the pleasant breath
  Of many a sylvan scene,—
They tell of sweet and sunny vales,
  And woodlands wildly green;
Ye cheer the lonely heart of age,—
  Ye fill the exile's dreams
With hope and home and memory,—
  Ye unforgotten streams:

Too soon the blessed springs of love
  To bitter fountains turn,
And deserts drink the stream that flows
  From hope's exhaustless urn;
And faint, upon the waves of life,
  May fall the summer beams,—
But they linger long and bright with you,
  Ye sweet unchanging streams!

The bards— the ancient bards—who sang
  When thought and song were new,
O, mighty waters! did they learn
  Their minstrelsy from you?

---

* Author of the beautiful poem—" Songs of our land," and of a volume of poems published in 1838. She was born in a small village, County Donegal in 1816. She lost her sight at the age of 18 months, and never recovered it.

  We give the above poem as well for its intrinsic excellence, as for the fact that Ireland is especially the land of streams and rivers. Most of our readers will recollect the beautiful and touching "rhapsody on rivers" in John Mitchel's *Jail Journal*.

For still, methinks, your voices blend
    With all their glorious themes,
That flow for ever fresh and free
    As the eternal streams!

Well might the sainted seer of old,
    Who trod the tearless shore,
Like many waters deem the voice
    The angel hosts adore!
For still, where deep the rivers roll,
    Or far the torrent gleams,
Our spirits hear the voice of God,
    Amid the rush of streams!

THE GARDENS OF LIFE.

H. SIGERSON.

I wandered, once, in a garden fair,
Bright were the flowers that blossomed there,
And a honied breath had the golden air!

And O! the sweet music that floated round,
Ever—ever—with magic sound,
Holding my sense in enchantment bound!

And One there dwelt in that land with me,
O! a peerless prince—a king was he!
His eyes made such light in this heart of mine,
That I thought 'twas *he* made the sun to shine.

And when we sat by the singing river,
I thought 'twas his voice that was sounding ever;
In the trembling shade when we sank to rest,
My heart seem'd throbbing within his breast!

But a shapeless Horror, dark as Death,
Came there with chill and deadly breath,
And turned to stone his eyes of light—
His love-warm lips, and forehead bright.

I pressed with kisses warm and sweet,
His icy hands and clay-cold feet—
But froze on my lips my kisses sweet.

Then stricken down on the earth I lay,
My pale brow pressed to the cold damp clay;
To the pulseless, dull, unfriendly breast
Of the cruel Earth, were my cold lips pressed.

Long, long I lay in that trance of pain,
While the fangs of death seemed to gnaw my brain
With a bitter woe, like the curse of Cain.

How long, alas! I cannot tell,
Nor what to that fair land befel,
For when I rose, with sudden start,
Urged by a fierce hope in my heart—

That all had been, not as it seemed—
That I had dreamed!—that I had dreamed
And that I still might live, and rest
On the dear heaven of his breast,
For ever, ever, ever blest!

I looked—and ah! I found him gone,
And I in a bleak wild alone;
No flowers were there, but foulest weeds,
And poisoned thorns, and tangled reeds.

And serpents writhing on the ground,
And ghastly phantoms hissing round,
And mocking me with hideous sound.

I turned to fly—but where?—oh, where?
For mocking spectres filled the air,
With horrors round me, every where.

Through briers and fen—through storm and sleet,
I hurried on, with bleeding feet;
O'er cruel crags and thorns I fled,
Scared by the terrors round me spread.

Led by dim lightning's fitful ray,
Until a black arch closed my way;
I grateful sighed, with failing breath—
"This is the blesséd gate of Death!"

And sinking down by that portal grim,
I wept, and wept till my eyes grew dim,
'Till my soul was faint, and my eyes were dim.

But while I wept, with solemn sound
The Ebon portal was unbound,
And slowly opened to my gaze
Long, silent aisles, in gloomy maze

And a soft voice, serene and mild,
Murmured,—"Come in, poor child!—poor child!
No mocking fiends shall haunt thee here;
Enter this temple without fear!"

It was a lady—sadly she
Was robed in sable drapery;
But in her eyes, serenely bright,
There beamed a sacred, calm delight,

Though dimmed with tears of pity mild,
While still she sighed—"Poor child!—poor child!"

I followed her, with trembling strength,
Through aisles of dim and solemn length,

Scarce heeding, as I totter'd slow,
Half blind with tears, half dead with woe,
The words of love, that, pure from GOD,
Fell from her lips, as on we trod.

And once I turned again to fly,
And to her gentle words did cry—
"O, let me see him, ere I die!"

"Child—child—*he never* was," she said;
"An empty dream in fancy bred,
Is all that's gone—is all thy loss."—
"O, bitter—bitter—bitter loss"
I sighed, "My peace, my hope is lost,
My joy is lost—all—all is lost!"

"O, child of GOD! there still is thine,
A treasured gift of love divine,
An offering meet for GOD's own shrine!
Then let thy vain lamenting cease,
This is the holy fane of peace;
Its gardens lead to Heaven's gate,
Where angels for thy coming wait!"

And—while she spoke—there seemed to rise
A light like that in dying eyes,
When, hands to weeping friends still given,
The *eyes* reflect the light of Heaven!

It seemed, as still it broader grew,
When near a portal wide we drew,
To close around my listening soul,
And pain, and memory's self control.

All life, save faith and love, seemed gone,
While strains of music drew me on
To where soft breezes kissed my brow,
Laden from many a drooping bough

Of clustering blossoms pure and bright,
Out in that wondrous, lovely light,
Where now I stand—where now I kneel—
While soft dews round me seem to steal,

More sweet than honey-dripping flowers
That blossomed in my own lost bowers;
No red rose here—but lilies white,
Which sway and tremble like the light
Of harvest moon on rippling waves,
Or pure souls, gliding from their graves!

Bowed by the weight of glory round,
Mute in a trance of love profound,
Upon the dewy moss I knelt,
When on my brow a hand I felt,

And sweetly did the lady say—
"O, child, beloved of heaven! stay,
Oh, stay! and far from passion's lure,
Dwell in this garden calm and pure!
Its fair paths lead to Heaven's gate,
Where angels for thy coming wait—
Stay and in sacred peace remain
Where sorrow shall not wound again."

O, far the passionate past above
I found that lily land of love!

BOATMAN'S HYMN.

From the Irish.

SAMUEL FERGUSSON, TRANSLATOR.

Bark that bear me through foam and squall,
You in the storm are my castle wall;
Though the sea should redden from bottom to top,
From tiller to mast she takes no drop.
   On the tide top, the tide top,
   Wherry aroon, my land and store!
   On the tide top, the tide top,
   She is the boat can sail go leór!

She dresses herself, and goes gliding on,
Like a dame in her robes of the Indian lawn;
For God has blessed her, gunnel and wale—
And oh! if you saw her stretch out to the gale,
   On the tide top, the tide top, etc.

Whillan,* ahoy! old heart of stone,
Stooping so black o'er the beach alone,
Answer me well—on the bursting brine
Saw you ever a bark like mine?
   On the tide top, the tide top, etc.

Says Whillan—"since first I was made of stone,
I have looked abroad o'er the beach alone—
But till to-day, on the bursting brine,
Saw I never a bark like thine."
   On the tide top, the tide top, etc.

* Whillan, a rock on the shore near Blacksod harbour.

God of the air! the seamen shout,
When they see us tossing the brine about:
Give us the shelter of strand or rock,
Or through and through us she goes with a shock!
    On the tide top, the tide top, etc.

A PICTURE OF MUNSTER.

Thomas Irwin.

Let the pilgrim of Beauty roam on as he may,
  From the snows of the north to the regions of wine,
What space can unfold in the light of the day,
  In glories more varied, sweet province, than thine?

Where the sun that at morn scatters fire on the crest
  Of the giant-browed Galtees, rounds southward, and takes
A golden farewell, ere he sinks to his nest
  In the arbutus bowers of the legended lakes.—

Here grey castles moulder like dreams of the past,
  'Mid the sunshine of morn and the dews of the clime;
Here round towers, haunted with shadows, still last
  On the evening inland, like dials of Time.

Streams freshen the meadows by forests of green,
  By moss-covered Abbeys, all ruined and bare,
Whose lone chancel casements at twilight are seen
  Like skeleton hands pointed heavenward in prayer:—

Here rise the great hills from the pasturing plains—
  Here goldens the cornland by village and lea—
Here rolls the broad Shannon, enriched with the
    rains,
  By the turrets of Limerick, swift to the sea.

Ah! once by those waters great argosies cast
  From their broad vans at sunset, a heroic gloom:
Ah! once by those mouldering battlements, past
  The dusky browed Spaniard in armour and
    plume:—

The pageant is o'er, but the blood that enshades
  The peasant's rich cheek from that fountain is
    drawn,
And glows in the dewy-dark eyes of her maids,
  Like the sunned Guadelquiver's first ripple at
    dawn.

Here feasted the chiefs by the castle's broad fire,
  And swelled the wild song of the wandering
    guest,
"Till the memoried music he struck from his lyre,
  Stirred the sword in the scabbard, the heart in
    the breast.

Here oft' as the battle day gloomed o'er the flood,
  Their fierce cheers gave note of the enemy's flight,
As they marched by the turrets of Desmond's wild
    wood,
  With their reddened spears raised in the even-
    ing light.

But lo ! while we muse in the light of thy streams,
 That sparkle in fresh diamond dances anigh,
The souls of thy clime, like a splendour in dreams,
 Descend in a radiant train from the sky.

Floats up from the Shannon a shadowy blast,
 Where great Brian's Kincora lies ruined and lone,
And a phantom looks down from the clouds of the past,
 And mournfully sighs on the years that are gone,

When discord lay dead as his steel-shining hand
 Waved the terror-struck fleets of the Northmen away;
When Peace-crownéd Victory shone in the land
 Like a warrior's ploom on a mid-summer day.

Rude years, but ennobled by battle and toil,
 Proud years, that still rise o'er the ages at rest,
Like turrets that look o'er a fertilised soil,
 As they moulder in mist on the skirt of the west.

And mark, after long barren ages of gloom,
 A new light burns broad on eternity's wing,
And Grattan strides proudly by Liberty's tomb,
 With the tongue of a prophet, the brain of a king :

Great chieftain of Freedom, proud Erinn's alone,
 Whose soul like a thunder-cloud born in the blue,
Could shake to its centre the foreigner's throne,
 While it nurtured the sweet native green with its dew.

Who treads by his side o'er the purple-belled heath,
  With wild scattered hair o'er that forehead so wan,
Whence flashes the upturned eye from its sheath,
  With a glance like the brown-hooded falcon's at dawn?—

Ah rich native Fancy, thy flame never lit
  Such splendours as swarmed from our Curran's bright brain—
Scintillant as spar, to the sparkle of wit,
  Yet soft as the blossom enriched with the rain.

Orphan Isle of the Ocean! how bright is thy sway,
  Though sadly thou sit'st by the western wave,
When the song of thy Moore charms the world on its way,
  When the brain of thy Burke rules the age from his grave.

Ah! when shall thy Genius arise with the power
  To guide thy old storms o'er a fertilized mould,
Pile them high in the west in tranquility's hour,
  And magic their gloom to a glory of gold.

Despair not—though shadowed by memory long,
  Great spirits shall guard thee like planets of flame:
And armoured by heaven, prolific and strong,
  With the youth of eternity toil for thy fame:

Yes, nurtured to life by the sun of thy clime,
  New heroes shall pace where thy Glories have trod,
And Voices, yet hushed in the silence of Time,
  Roll up with thine old living echoes, to God.

A PORTRAIT.

GERALD GRIFFIN.

Life is like a glass, o'er whose surface gleaming,
Brilliant shadows pass, but vain as childhood's dreaming.
Could we find the art to fix the flying splendour,
ONE, I know, my heart never would surrender.

'Tis a lovely Shade! paint it while it lingers,
Ere it fail and fade; ere the wasting fingers
Of the haggard Time—the blasting and consuming—
Touch its tender prime, and wither all its blooming.

Paint a blooming cheek, filled with healthful beauty,
Ready smiles that speak of peace and cherished duty;
Eyes that shift and shine with a deep full meaning;
Clouded curls that twine, a sunny forehead screening.

Paint a blooming lip, with blushing softness swelling;
Where mirth and kindness keep an undivided dwelling:
The charm is wanting still that on the soft lip lingers,
And the ready skill that haunts those taper fingers.

Merry hours will fleet, friends that love must sever,
Oft in joy we meet, to part, in tears, for ever!
But, in absence, warm, upon this heart reclining,
I will keep that form of memory's fond designing.

THE BROTHERS:
HENRY AND JOHN SHEARS.*

LADY WILDE.†

'Tis midnight, falls the lamp-light dull and sickly
    On a pale and anxious crowd,
Through the court, and round the judges, thronging
    thickly,
    With prayers they dare not speak aloud.
Two youths, two noble youths, stand prisoners at
    the bar—
    You can see them through the gloom—
In the pride of life and manhood's beauty, there
    they are,
    Awaiting their death-doom:

All eyes an earnest watch on these are keeping,
    Some sobbing, turn away,
And the strongest men can hardly see for weeping,
    So noble and so loved were they.
Their hands are locked together, these young
    brothers,
    As before the judge they stand;
They feel not the deep grief that moves the others;
    For they die for Fatherland.

---

* Born in Cork. Their father was a banker in that city, where his leisure moments were devoted to literary and benevolent pursuits.

Glasheen, about a mile from the city, was his country residence, where his children were reared. The brothers were arrested on the 21st May, 1798; tried on the 12th, and executed on the 14th of July following, with circumstances of cruelty and barbarity.

† Wife of Sir Wm. Wilde, physician and *savant*, of Dublin. This lady is author of many beautiful poems, and translator of several works from the German.

They are pale, but it is not fear that whitens
   On each proud high brow,
For the triumph of the martyr's glory brightens
   Around them even now.
They sought to free their land from thrall of
   stranger,
   Was it treason? Let them die;
But their blood will cry to heaven—the Avenger
   Yet will hearken from on high.

Before them, shrinking, cowering, scarcely human,
   The base informer bends,
Who, Judas-like, could sell the blood of true men,
   While he clasped their hands as friends.
Ay; could fondle the young children of his
   victim
   Break bread with his young wife,
At the moment that, for gold, his perjured dictum
   Sold the husband and the father's life.

There is silence in the midnight—eyes are keeping
   Troubled watch, till forth the jury come;
There is silence in the midnight—eyes are weep-
   ing—
   Guilty! is the fatal doom.
For a moment, o'er the brothers' noble faces,
   Came a shadow sad to see,
Then, silently, they rose up in their places,
   And embraced each other fervently.

Oh! the rudest heart might tremble at such
   sorrow,
   The rudest cheek might blush at such a scene;

Twice the judge essayed to speak the word—
  to-morrow—
  Twice faltered, as a woman he had been.
To-morrow! Fain the elder would have spoken,
  Prayed for respite, though it is not death he
    fears;
But thoughts of home and wife his heart hath
    broken,
  And his words are stopped by tears.
But the youngest—oh! he speaks out bold and
    clearly;
  "I have no ties of children or of wife;
Let me die—but spare the brother, who more
    dearly
  Is loved by me than life."
Pale martyrs, ye may cease, your days are num-
    bered;
  Next noon your sun of life goes down;
One day between the sentence and the scaffold;
  One day between the torture and the crown.

A hymn of joy is rising from creation;
  Bright the azure of the glorious summer sky;
But human hearts weep sore in lamentation,
  For the brothers are led forth to die.
Ay; guard them with your cannon and your
    lances—
  So of old came martyrs to the stake;
Ay; guard them—see the people's flashing glances,
  For those noble two are dying for their sake.

Yet none spring forth their bonds to sever;
  Ah! methinks had I been there,

I'd have dared a thousand deaths ere ever
    The sword should touch their hair.*
It falls!—there is a shriek of lamentation
    From the weeping crowd around;
They are stilled—the noblest hearts within the
    nation—
    The noblest heads lie bleeding on the ground.

Years have passed since that fatal scene of dying,
    † Yet life-like to this day,
In their coffins still those severed heads are lying,
    Kept by angels from decay.
Oh! they preach to us, those still and pallid
    features;
    Those pale lips yet implore us from their graves,
To strive for our birthright as God's creatures,
    Or die, if we can but live as slaves.

---

* Lady Wilde gave proof of her high-mindedness in 'Forty-Eight: standing up in the gallery of the court, she announced herself before the judges of the land, the author of an article, which was then being adduced as proof of the guilt of the Editor of one of the National Papers.

† It is a most curious circumstance that the bodies of these two martyrs have not mouldered into corruption, but by some singularly preservative quality of the air of the vault in St. Michan's Church, Dublin, are in preservation to this day.

BURNING OF AN EMIGRANT SHIP.

STREET BALLAD.

Come all ye Irish people,
    And hear my mournful theme;
While I relate our hardships great
    Upon the watery main:
The fourth day of September,
    For New York did we set sail,
On board the ship the " Austria,"
    With a sweet and pleasant gale.

Six hundred souls we had on board,
    Both passengers and crew;
For nine long days we ploughed the seas,
    Right well the wind it blew,
Until this dreadful fire took place,
    With flames that raged all round—
Four hundred souls were burned,
    Or in the cold sea drown'd!

Our captain when the fire burst forth
    " O, Lord, we're lost!" he cried,
And to escape the raging flames
    Plunged wildly in the tide!
O, God, the cries of children dear!
    The blazing pitchy seams:
The mother's bitter tears could not
    Subdue the cruel flames!

The most of these were emigrants
  From Galway's pleasant strand;
From racking tyrant landlords,
  They quit their native land;
In hope to live more happily
  'Mong strangers far away,
They bent their course to New York,
  All on this woful day.

The cries of these poor passengers
  Would pierce your heart with grief;
All shrieking on the burning deck
  So vainly for relief;
The mothers to their children clung,
  " O, we may rue the day
We left out poor old Ireland,
  For countries far away!"

Their bitter groans and sufferings
  Would pierce your very heart,
Without a spot to shun the flames
  Or bid their fate depart;
They lost their lives and property,
  In flames and in the waves;
And not a mass was offer'd up
  Above their lonely graves!

O, neighbours dear, O, Irishmen,
  Let every Christian pray,
That God will rid our native land
  Of racking landlord sway;
And as these banish'd people did,
  In awful sufferings, die,—
God grant them sweet salvation
  With His Dear Son on High!

F

BY MEMORY INSPIRED.
STREET BALLAD.*
Air.—"Cruiskeen Lan."

By Memory inspired
And love of country fired,
The deeds of MEN I love to dwell upon;
And the patriotic glow
Of my Spirit must bestow
A tribute to O'Connell that is gone, boys, gone,!
Here's a memory to the friends that are gone.

In October 'Ninety-Seven—
May his soul find rest in Heaven—
William Orr to execution was led on:
The jury, drunk, agreed
That IRISH was his creed:
For perjury and threats drove them on, boys, on:
Here's the memory of John Mitchell that is gone!

In 'Ninety-Eight—the month July—
The informer's pay was high;
When Reynolds gave the gallows brave MacCann;
But MacCann was Reynolds' first—
One could not allay his thirst;
So he brought up Bond and Byrne that are gone, boys, gone:
Here's the memory of the friends that are gone!

* We have copied this from a broad sheet which we found hawking about the country; headed with a rude woodcut of two men leaning pensively on a table, and a standing cavalier, with a glass in one hand and bottle in the other, supposed to be engaged singing to them the above patriotic song.

      We saw a nation's tears
      Shed for John and Henry Shears;
Betrayed by Judas, Captain Armstrong;
      We may forgive, but yet
      We never can forget
The poisoning of Maguire that is gone, boys, gone:
Our high Star and true Apostle that is gone!

      How did Lord Edward die?
      Like a man, without a sigh;
But he left his handiwork on Major Swan!
      But Sirr, with steel-clad breast,
      And coward heart at best,
Left us cause to mourn Lord Edward that is gone, boys, gone:
Here's the memory of our friends that are gone!

      September, Eighteen-three,
      Closed this cruel history,
When Emmet's blood the scaffold flowed upon:
      O, had their spirits been wise,
      They might then realise
Their freedom—but we drink to Mitchel that is gone, boys, gone:
Here's the memory of the friends that are gone.

A CUSHLA GAL MO CHREE.*
Michael Doheny.

The long, long wished-for hour has come,
  Yet come, astor, in vain;
And left thee but the wailing hum
  Of sorrow and of pain:
My light of life—my lonely love!
  Thy portion sure must be,
Man's scorn below, God's wrath above—
  A cuisle geal mo croide!†

---

* Doubtless "Duffy's Ballad Poetry of Ireland," which, in less than a month, ran through three editions, is known and prized in the cottages of the farmers. But even amongst the poorer labouring classes of the country, this love for, and appreciation of some of the refined ballads is to be met with. Evidence of this is recorded in "Memorandums in Ireland," a work written by Doctor Forbes, one of the Physicians to the Queen, who seems a man capable of recording truly what he saw. He introduces the above ballad with these words, "Our driver from Kenmare to Killarney, a tectotaller, was a true son of Saint Patrick. He volunteered a song, and made the echoes ring with his sonorous strains. One of his songs was really in itself a song of no ordinary beauty and pathos; and when it was considered under what circumstances it had been written, and that it now burst forth spontaneously, and, as it were, irresistibly, from the lips of this young Irish peasant, amid the very scenes where it had been composed, it could not fail being listened to with redoubled interest." * * * A reward of £300 was offered for his (Michael Doheny's) apprehension, but none of his countrymen, however poor or wretched were found mercenary enough to earn it; and he finally succeeded in making his escape from Cork. * * * It was evident that our minstrel,

† *A cushla gal mochree*, O bright pulse of my heart.

I've given Thee manhood's early prime,
    And manhood's teeming years ;
I've blessed Thee in my merriest time,
    And shed with Thee my tears ;
And, mother, though thou cast away
    The child who'd die for Thee,
My fondest wishes still should pray
    For cuisle geal mo croide !

For Thee I've tracked the mountain's sides,
    And slept within the brake,
More lonely than the swan that glides
    O'er Lua's fairy lake.
The rich have spurned me from their door,
    Because I'd make Thee free,
Yet still I love Thee more and more,
    A cuisle geal mo croide !

I've run the Outlaw's wild career,
    And borne his load of ill ;
His rocky couch—his dreamy fear—
    With fixed sustaining will ;

though a very indifferent singer, felt the pathos of his song; and it soon appeared that his sympathies were strongly on the same side as those of its author. On my asking him, if he would have joined in this insurrection if he had come in the way of it, he replied instantly, ' to be sure I would, a man ought to fight for his country.' So true it is," goes on this English writer to say, " that there still dwells deep in the Irish mind the memory of the ancient independence and legendary glories of Ireland ; and the notion of something being yet due in the shape of vengeance on the sons of the conquerors."

And should his last dark chance befall,
    Even that shall welcome be;
In Death I'd love Thee best of all,
    A cuisle geal mo croide!

'Twas prayed for thee, the world around,
    'Twas hoped for thee, by all,
That with one gallant sunward bound,
    Thou'dst burst long ages' thrall;
Thy faith was tried alas! and those
    Who'd peril all for thee,
Were curs'd and branded as thy foes,
    A cuisle geal mo croide!

What fate is thine, unhappy Isle,
    When even the trusted few
Would pay thee back with hate and guile,
    When most they should be true;
'Twas not my strength or spirit fail'd,
    Or those who'd die for thee,
Who lov'd Thee truly have not fail'd,
    A cuisle geal mo croide!

LAMENT OF THE EJECTED IRISH PEASANT.*

ANONYMOUS.

Air.—"Eileen Aroon."

The night is dark and dreary,
    A gradh geal mo chroide:†
And the heart that loves you weary,
    A gradh geal mo chroide;

* Von Raumer, making a Tour in Ireland, tries to explain to his own country people the state of things

† *A hrau gal mochree,* O bright love of my heart.

For every hope is blighted,
That bloomed when first we plighted
Our troth, and were united,
    A gradh geal mo chroide!

Still our homestead we behold,
    A gradh geal mo chroide;
But the cheerful hearth is cold,
    A gradh geal mo chroide;
And those around its glow,
Assembled long ago,
In the cold, cold earth lie low,
    A gradh geal mo chroide!

'Twas famine's wasting breath,
    A gradh geal mo chroide;
That wing'd the shaft of death,
    A gradh geal mo chroide;
And the landlord lost to feeling,
Who drove us from our sheeling,
Though we prayed for mercy kneeling,
    A gradh geal mo chroide!

produced by the Landlord Land-laws of this country; thus :—" How shall I translate *tenant-at-will?* Shall I say *serfs?* No, in feudal times, serfdom consisted rather in keeping the vassals attached to the soil and, by no means in driving them away. An ancient vassal is a lord compared with the present tenant-at-will, to whom the law affords no defence. Why not call them *Wegjagdbare* (chaseable)? · But this difference lessens this analogy—that for hares, stags, and deer, there is a season during which no one is allowed to hunt them—whereas tenants-at-will are hunted all the year round. And if anyone would defend his farm (as badgers and foxes are allowed to defend their cover) it is here denominated 'rebellion!'"

Oh! 'twas heartless from that floor,
    A gradh geal mo chroide;
Where our fathers dwelt of yore,
    A gradh geal mo chroide;
To fling our offspring—seven—
'Neath the wintry skies of heaven,
To perish on that even',
    A gradh geal mo chroide!

But the sleety blast blows chill,
    A gradh geal mo chroide;
Let me press thee closer still,
    A gradh geal mo chroide,
To this scathed bleeding heart,
Beloved as thou art,
For too soon—too soon we part,
    A gradh geal mo chroide!

THE BATTLE OF ARDNOCHER; 1328.*
MacGeoghegan.†

On the eve of St. Laurance,
At the cross of Glenfad,

---

* "A.D. 1328.—Mac Geoghegan gave a great overthrow to the English, in which three thousand five hundred of them, together with the De Altons, were slain. This battle, in which the English forces met with such tremendous defeat, was fought near Mullingar, on the day before the feast of St. Laurance, namely, the 9th August. The Irish clans were commanded by William Mac Geoghegan, Lord of Kinel Fiacha, in Westmeath, comprising the present baronies of Moycashel and Rathconrath. The English forces were commanded by Lord Thomas Butler, the Petits, Tuites, Nagles, Delemeres, etc. The battle took place at the hill of Ardnocher."—*An. Four Masters.*

† Author of "The Monks of Kilcrea."

Both of chieftains and bonaghts,
  What a muster we had!
Thick as bees, round the heather,
  On the side of Slieve Bloom,
To the trysting they gather
  By the light of the moon.

For the Butler from Ormond,
  With a hosting he came,
And harried Moycashel
  With havoc and flame;
Not a hoof or a hayrick,
  Nor corn-blade to feed on,
Had he left on the wide land
  Right up to Dunbreedon.

Then gathered MacGeoghegan,
  The high prince of Donore,
With O'Connor from Croghan,
  And O'Dempsys galore;
And, my soul, how we shouted,
  As dashed in with their men,
Bold Mac Coghlan from Clara,
  O'Molloy from the glen.

And not long did we loiter,
  Where the four toghers meet,
But his saddle each tightened,
  And his spurs closer set,
By the skylight that flashes
  All their red burnings back,
And by black gore and ashes
  Fast the rievers we track.

Till we came to Arnocher,
  And its steep slope we gain,
And stretched there beneath us,
  Saw their host in the plain;
And high shouted our leader
  ('Twas the brave William Roe)—
" By the red hand of Niall,
  'Tis the Sassenach foe!

" Now, low level your spears,
  Grasp each battle-axe firm,
And for God and our Ladye,
  Strike ye downright and stern;
For our homes and our altars
  Be ye steadfast and true,
And our watchword be vengeance,
  And Lamh Dearg Aboo!"*

Oh, then down like a torrent
  With a " farra!" we swept,
And full stout was the Saxon,
  Who his saddle-tree kept;
For we dashed through their horsemen
  Till they reeled from the stroke,
And their spears, like dry twigs,
  With our axes we broke.

With our plunder we found them,
  Our fleet garrons and kine,
And each chalice and cruet
  They had snatched from God's shrine;
But a red debt we paid them,
  The Sassenach raiders,
As we scattered their spearsmen,
  Slew chieftains and leaders.

* *Lauv djarrig aboo*, the Red Hand for ever.

In the Pale there is weeping
  And watching in vain.
De Lacy and De Alton,
  Can ye reckon your slain?
Where's your chieftain, fierce Nagle?
  Has De Netterville fled?
Ask the Molingar eagles,
  Whom their carcases fed.

Ho! ye riders from Ormond,
  Will ye brag in your hall,
How your lord was struck down
  With his mail'd knights and all?
Swim at midnight the Shannon,
  Beard the wolf in his den,
Ere you ride to Moycashel
  On a foray again!

THE YOUNG ENTHUSIAST.

THOMAS FRANCIS MEAGHER.

Though young that heart, though free each thought,
  Though free and wild each feeling,
And though with fire each dream be fraught
  Across those bright eyes stealing—

That heart is true, those thoughts are bold,
  And bold each feeling sweepeth;
There lies not there a bosom cold,
  A pulse that faintly sleepeth.

His dreams are idiot-dreams, ye say,
    The dreams of fairy story;
Those dreams will burn in might one day,
    And flood his path with glory!

Thou old dull vassal! fling thy sneer
    Upon that young heart coldly,
And laugh at deeds *thy* heart may fear,
    Yet *he* will venture boldly.

Ay, fling thy sneer while dull and slow
    Thy withered blood is creeping;
That heart will beat, *that* spirit glow,
    When thy tame pulse is sleeping.

Ay, laugh when o'er his country's ills
    With manly eye he weepeth;
Laugh, when his brave heart throbs and thrills,
    And thy cold bosom sleepeth.

Laugh, when he vows in Heaven's sight,
    Ne'er to flinch—ne'er to falter;
To toil and fight for a nation's right,
    And guard old Freedom's altar.

Ay, laugh when on the fiery wing
    Of hero thought ascending
To fame's bold cliff with eagle spring,
    That young bright mind is tending.

He'll gain that cliff, he'll reach that throne,
    The throne where genius shineth,
When round and through thy nameless stone,
    The green weed thickly twineth.

MUSIC, MUSIC, COME, OH! COME.*

Isaac Stephen Varian.†

Music, music, come, oh come!
From thy lone retreat, in the forest deep;
From thy crystal throne, where the wild waves
    sweep;
From thy seat, at eve, by the mountain's rill;
From thy cave, where the lightnings work their will:
Come, sweep o'er our souls,—in our bosoms thrill!

"Thou hast called; what strain would'st thou hear?
    Has affliction thy calm spirit broken,
Shall we breathe tones of love in thine ear,
    Or shall wild notes of gladness be spoken?
Thou hast called; what strain would'st thou hear?"

Sing to me; I am sad, and alone,
    Bereavement has weighed down my soul,
From Erinn the loved ones are gone,
    My crushed spirit would feel thy controul;
Sing to me; I am sad, and alone,

Sing to me, in the music of love,
    As it breathes o'er the opening flowers,
And let Hope, like the wing of the dove,
    Waft my soul to its shadowy bowers;
Sing to me, in the music of love.

---

* Has been set to music, as a Glee for four voices, with Pianoforte accompaniment, by Abel Wadsworth Deane, Esq.—can be had of J. A. Novello, 69 Dean-street, Soho: also in New York at 389, Broadway.

† Of Cork—now of Talbot-street, Dublin.

Sing to me, for my heart would rejoice,
  My spirit is joyous and free,
And the tones I would hear from thy voice,
  Are the echoes of gladness and glee;
Sing to me, for my heart would rejoice.

" Then, listen ! I have notes that can cheer
  The heart, when 'tis sad, and alone ;
That pour Hope in the Patriot's ear,
  And echo to gaiety's tone ;
Then, listen ; when music is near !

THE BOYS OF WEXFORD.
Street Ballad.
ROBERT DWYER JOYCE.
Air—" The Boys of Wexford."

In comes the captain's daughter,—
  The captain of the Yeos,
Saying, " Brave United man,
  We'll ne'er again be foes.
A thousand pounds I'll give you,
  And fly from home with thee,
And dress myself in man's attire,
  And fight for libertie !"
    We are the boys of Wexford,
      Who fought with heart and hand
    To burst in twain the galling chain,
      And free our native land !

And when we left our cabins, boys,
  We left with right good will,
To see our friends and neighbours
  That were at Vinegar Hill !

A young man from our ranks,
   A cannon he let go:
He slapt it into Lord Mountjoy—
   A tyrant he laid low!
    We are the boys of Wexford,
      Who fought with heart and hand
    To burst in twain the galling chain.
    And free our native land!

We bravely fought and conquered
   At Ross, and Wexford town,
And, if we failed to keep them,
   'Twas drink that brought us down.
We had no drink beside us
   On Tubber'neering's day,
Depending on the long bright pike,
   And well it worked its way!
    We are the boys of Wexford,
      Who fought with heart and hand
    To burst in twain the galling chain,
    And free our native land!

They came into the country
   Our blood to waste and spill;
But let them weep for Wexford,
   And think of Oulart Hill!
'Twas drink that still betrayed us—
   Of them we had no fear,
For every man could do his part
   Like Forth and Shelmalier!
    We are the boys of Wexford,
      Who fought with heart and hand
    To burst in twain the galling chain
    And free our native land!

My curse upon all drinking!
　It made our hearts full sore,
For bravery won each battle,
　But drink lost evermore;
And if for want of leaders
　We lost at Vinegar Hill,
We're ready for another fight,
　And love our country still!
　　We are the boys of Wexford,
　　　Who fought with heart and hand
　　To burst in twain the galling chain,
　　　And free our native land!

THE FELONS.

John T. Campion:[*]

[When Thomas Francis Meagher and two more of the 'Forty-Eight men were outlawed wanderers in Tipperary, and at the close of a weary evening, sought food and shelter from a peasant whom they met on the way, the colloquy and events of the ballad took place.]

"Good peasant—we are strangers, here,
　And night is gathering fast;
The stars scarce glimmer in the sky;
　And moans the mountain's blast;
Can'st tell us of a place to rest?
　We're wearied with the road;
No churl the peasant used to be
　With homely couch and food."

[*] Of King's Bridge, Kilkenny.

" I cannot help myself nor know
  Where ye may rest or stay ;
A few more hours, the moon will shine,
  And light you on your way."

" But peasant—can you let a man
  Appeal to you in vain ;
Here at your very cabin door ;
  And 'mid the pelting rain ?
Here in the dark, and in the night,
  Where one scarce sees a span ;
What !— close your heart !—and close your door !
  And be an Irishman ?"

" No—no—go on—the moon will rise
  In a short hour or two :
What can a peaceful labourer say ?
  Or a poor toiler do ?"

" You're poor ?—well—here's a golden chance
  To make you rich and great !
Five hundred pounds are on our heads !
  The gibbet is our fate !
Fly—raise the cry, and win the gold !
  Or some may cheat you soon ;
And we'll abide, by the road side,
  And wait the rising moon."

What ails the peasant ?—does he flush
  At the wild greed of gold ?
Why seizes he the wanderers' hands ?—
  Hark to his accents bold : —

"Ho! I *have* a heart for you, neighbours!
  Ay—and a hearth, and a home!—
Ay, and a help for you neighbours!
  God bless ye—and prosper ye—come!

"Come—out of the light of the soldiers;
  Come in 'mongst the children and all;
And I'll guard ye, for sake of old Ireland;
  Till Connall, himself gets a fall.

"To the devil, with all their gold guineas,
  Come in—everything is your own—
And I'll kneel at your feet—friends of Ireland!
  What I wouldn't for king on his throne.

"God bless ye that stood in the danger,
  In the midst of the country's mishap;
That stood up to meet the big famine;
  Och!—ye are the men in the gap!

"Come in—with a 'Cead Mille Failthe;'
  Sit down; and don't make any noise;
Till I come for more comforts to crown ye;
  Till I gladden the hearts of the boys!

"Arrah! shake hands again—noble fellows!
  That left your own homes for the poor!
Not a man in the land could betray you,
  Or shut up his heart or his door!"

LOVE IN THE COUNTRY.

John T. Campion.

Have you seen my sweetheart
   Passing on the way?
Like a hill-side sun-gleam,
   On a harvest day.
Such fine eyes of hazel!
   Such dark flowing hair!
Like a graceful cloud-wreath
   Leaning on the air.

Saw you the white foam-hill
   Sailing down the Nore?
How amid the rushes
   Flowing near the shore,
In, it steers and nestles—
   Takes its downy rest:—
So my sweetheart's bosom
   Hides beneath her vest

Saw you the wild mushroom
   As you slowly pass—
Like a pearly dawning,
   Bedded in the grass?
So in her dark buskin,
   Lies my sweetheart's foot,
Locked up, like the kernel
   In the tuckered nut!

Have you seen my sweetheart
   When she speaks or sings?
Lo! the birds of Eden
   With uplifted wings!

Warm—bright—and rosy—
  Dazzling white beneath,
Like her lips of crimson
  O'er their ivory wreath.

Have you seen my sweetheart,
  Blushing when we meet?
Looking mild and gentle,
  Speaking kind and sweet.
Earth were sad without her—
  Time no joy could bring—
Bright is all above her,
  Like one fairy ring;
Bless her eyes of hazel!
  Bless her flowing hair!
Like a graceful cloud-wreath
  Leaning on the air!

AN EXILE'S DREAMS.

Joseph Brenan.

I will go to holy Ireland,
  The land of Saint and Sage,
Where the pulse of boyhood is leaping
  In the shrunken form of Age;
Where the shadow of giant Hopes
  For evermore is cast,
And the wraiths of mighty chieftains
  Are looming through the Past.
From the cold land of the Stranger
  I will take my joyous flight,
To sit by my slumbering country,
  And watch her through the night;

When the Spring is in the sky,
   And the flowers are on the land,
I will go to ancient Ireland,
   Of the open heart and hand.

I will go where the Galtees,
   Are rising bare and high,
With their haggard foreheads fronting
   The scowl of the clouded sky;
I will gaze adown on the valleys,
   And bless the teeming sod,
And commune with the mountains—
   "The Almoners of God;"
I will list to the murmurous song
   Which is rising from the river,
Which flows, crooning to the Ocean,
   For ever and for ever.
When the May-month is come,
   When the year is fresh and young,
I will go to the home of my fathers—
   The land of sword and song.

I will go where Killarney
   Is sleeping in peaceful rest,
Unmoved, save when a falling leaf
   Ripples its placid breast;
Where the branches of oak and arbutus
   Are weaving a pleasant screen,
And the sunshine breaks in diamonds
   Through its tracery of green;
Where the mists, like fantastic spectres,
   For ever rise and fall,
And the rainbow of the Covenant
   Is spanning the mountains tall.

When the wind blows from the West,
    Across the deep Sea,
I will sail to my Innisfail,
    To the " Isle of Destiny."

I will go to beautiful Wicklow,
    The hunted outlaw's rest,
Which the tread of rebel and rapparee
    In many a struggle prest :
I will go to the lonely graveyard,
    Near the pleasant fields of Kildare,
And pray for my chief and my hero,
    Young Tone who is sleeping there :
I will go to the gloomy Thomas-street,
    Where gallant Robert died,
And to the grim St. Michan's,
    Where " the Brothers" lie side by side ;
I will go to where the heroes
    Of the Celts are laid,
And chant a *Miserere*
    For the souls of the mighty Dead.

I will seize my pilgrim staff,
    And cheerily wander forth
From the smiling face of the South
    To the black frown of the North ;
And in some hour of twilight
    I will mount the tall Slieve-Bloom,
And weave me a picture-vision
    In the evening's pleasant gloom :
I will call up the buried leaders
    Of the ancient Celtic race,
And gaze with a filial fondness
    On each sternly-noble face—

The masters of the mind,
  And the chieftains of the steel,
Young Carolan and Grattan,
  The M'Caura and O'Neil;
I will learn from their voices,
  With a student's love and pride,
To live as they lived,
  And to die as they died.
Oh, I will sail from the West,
  And never more will part
From the ancient home of my people—
  The land of the loving heart.*

THE SPINNING WHEEL.

John Francis Waller, LL.D.

Mellow the moonlight to shine is beginning,
Close by the window young Eileen is spinning;
Bent o'er the fire her blind grandmother, sitting,
Is croaning, and moaning, and drowsily knitting—
" Eileen, achora, I hear some one tapping."
" 'Tis the ivy, dear mother, against the glass flapping."
" Eily, I surely hear somebody sighing."
" 'Tis the sound, mother dear, of the summer wind dying."
  Merrily, cheerily, noiselessly whirring,
    Swings the wheel, spins the wheel, while the foot's stirring;
  Sprightly, and brightly, and airily ringing,
  Thrills the sweet voice of the young maiden singing.

* From the " American Review" 1851.

"What's that noise that I hear at the window, I
  wonder?"
"'Tis the little birds chirping the holly-bush under."
"What makes you be shoving and moving your
  stool on,
And singing, all wrong, that old song of 'The
  Coolan?'"
There's a form at the casement—the form of her
  truelove—
And he whispers, with face bent, "I'm waiting for
  you, love;
Get up on the stool, through the lattice step lightly,
We'll rove in the grove while the moon's shining
  brightly."
  Merrily, cheerily, noiselessly whirring, &c.

The maid shakes her head, on her lip lays her fingers,
Steals up from her seat—longs to go, and yet lingers;
A frightened glance turns to her drowsy grandmother,
Puts one foot on the stool, spins the wheel with the
  other.
Lazily, easily, swings now the wheel round,
Slowly and lowly is heard now the reel's sound;
Noiseless and light to the lattice above her
The maid steps—then leaps to the arms of her lover.
 Slower—and slower—and slower the wheel
   swings;
 Lower—and lower—and lower the reel rings;
 Ere the reel and the wheel stopped their ring-
   ing and moving,
 Through the grove the young lovers by moon-
   light are roving.

THE EVICTION.
Michael Seagrave.*

A wretched quilt and bed of straw—
   A shrunken Frame, and hoary hair;
Full eighty winters' snows she saw,
   Now famine's fever laid her there:
And Malachi, her boy, is gone
   Across the broad Atlantic wave;
A daughter of her eldest son
   Is left to see her in her grave.

A maiden purer than the glow
   That tints the snow when Spring is bright;
Now down her cheeks the hot tears flow,
   And she has watched the dreary night,
Oft startled by the dismal croak—
   The raven's and the banshee's cry;
Nor tasted sleep till daylight broke—
   O God, what horror meets her eye!

A band of ruffians burst the door,
   With huge crow-bar, and torch in hand,
Sent by their ruthless lord to clear
   The rightful owners off the land—
Whose muscles raised his fairy hall,
   Whose sweat increased his pampered pride;
Poor slaves! though they seemed happy all
   Before the former landlord died.

Now famine is the peasant's lot—
   And hear the hapless maiden pray
"For pity spare this humble cot
   Till that shrunk Form be laid in clay!"

* A working man, weaver by trade, an Irishman, residing in Barnsley, Yorkshire.

But " fire the thatch, the birds will fly!
   That landlord's cry, she hears no more;
The light has fled her once bright eye,
   And she sinks senseless on the floor.

*   *   *   *   *.

The people fly from hill and vale,
   While flames illuminate the sky,
And learn grim oppression's tale
   With fiery vengeance in each eye.
And foremost was a youth as brave
   As ever trod the earth before;
He raised her in his arms—" Oh, save—
   She's breathing now—she is no more!

" O speak, Kathleen, my darling bright,
   My own adored Cushla-ma-chree!
Ah, no, thy spirit's ta'en its flight!
   Revenge is all that's left to me."
" Oh, patience, youth," a voice now spoke,
   " To-night, at ten, we meet to try
The villain who has dealt death's stroke,
   And by God's light he'll surely die!"

The pale moon issued from a cloud,
   The earth received its murdered dead,
And paler than the victim's shroud
   The lover o'er the mountain sped—
A cavern reached—the jury there—
   The murderer is guilty found—
" Then ere to-morrow's sun, I swear
   To fell the tyrant to the ground!"

Now daylight bounds with happy speed,
   The hounds are panting for the chase;
His lordship on a prancing steed
   Comes forth—ha! who said " villian base!"

The dreaded voice rings in his ear—
"Vile murderer, thy day is o'er!"
The tyrant shakes with rage and fear—
And groans—and falls to rise no more

THE GREEN LITTLE SHAMROCK OF IRELAND

ANDREW CHERRY.[*]

There's a dear little plant that grows in our isle,
  'Twas Saint Patrick himself, sure, that set it;
And the sun of his labour with pleasure did smile,
  And with dew from his eye often wet it.
It thrives through the bog, through the brake,
    through the mireland:
And he called it the dear little shamrock of Ireland.
    The sweet little shamrock, the dear little
      shamrock,
    The sweet little, green little, shamrock of
      Ireland.

This dear little plant still grows in our land,
  Fresh and fair as the daughters of Erin,
Whose smiles can bewitch, whose eyes can command,
  In each climate that they may appear in;

---

[*] Born in Limerick, 1780. Wrote "The Bay of Biscay," and "Tom Moody,". Was manager of the London theatre in which Edmund Kean made his first appearance.

And shine through the bog, through the brake,
    through the mireland ;
Just like their own dear little shamrock of Ireland.
    The sweet little shamrock, the dear little
      shamrock,
      The sweet little, green little, shamrock of
      Ireland.

This dear little plant that springs from our soil,
    When its three little leaves are extended,
Denotes from one stalk we together should toil,
    And ourselves by ourselves be befriended ;
And still through the bog, through the brake,
    through the mireland,
From one root should branch, like the shamrock
    of Ireland.
    The sweet little shamrock, the dear little
      shamrock,
      The sweet little, green little, shamrock of
      Ireland.

THE BLARNEY STONE.

JOHN FITZGERALD.[*]

The Anglo-Irish tradition connected with the origin of the word "Blarney," as applied to an insinuating

[*] A wood-carver residing in Cork, supporting a large family by the labour of his hands.

and persuasive address is, that one of the chiefs of the district having visited the court of Queen Elizabeth for the purpose of making an appeal to her, urged his cause with so much tact and eloquence, that the Queen, on hearing the interpretation of his speech, turned to one of her courtiers and asked—"What part of Ireland is this goodly chieftain from?" and having been answered, "From Blarney," she ever after used the word, when any one of her courtiers sought by plausible representation to win her favour to their cause. The genuine Irish tradition connected with the stone is given in the following verses, by one, who has had it direct from the voices which were afloat upon the air, while he was reposing by the wooded shores of the waters near. Blarney was a place of note in the Druidical ages. A huge *Cromleac*, or Druid-altar, stands there still, in a space of wonderful beauty, a little below the *Witch's Stairs*—on the margin of the *com-an*. The Four Masters, at A. M. 3501, mention the *Carrac Blarne*, or Rock of Blarney. The stone usually appealed to now, by the touching of lips, is not the genuine stone. *That* lies much farther down, built in the walls of the castle: to kiss it, the neophyte must be lowered, head downwards, by ropes. So the late parish priest of Blarney, Father Horgan, used to say, and he was a man of great traditionary learning. Of course at the period to which the tradition refers, though only 700 years since, the waters of the Lee were far deeper than they are now, and shells of great size and splendour were abundant on the shore.

On a moss-clad stone by the sparkling Lee,
   In the mystic days of old,
Sat a being fair as the eye could see,
   Who played on a harp of gold;
And sang sweet music, soft and rare,
As the zephyrs tossed her flowing hair.

"Oh, come, young chieftain, come," she sang,
　"Thou art beautiful and brave,
And thy heart shall feel no grief or pang,
　In our home beneath the wave;
While thou art sitting by my side,
And the harp is touched by your fairy bride.

"The wealth of the ocean is at thy call
　In our fairy land of dreams,
Where age ne'er comes to fade or pall—
　And the music of fairy streams
Shall lull thee to sleep on thy flow'ry bed,
And the crown of our kingdom shall deck thy head.

"This land is lovely as aught on earth,
　But is nought compared to mine;
For sorrow tracks your love and mirth,
　And your light doth seldom shine."
"Hold! Fairy queen," and he raised his hand,
"Tis Erinn still, and my native land.

"I love its mountains, wild and free,
　Where shines the hand of God;
And, O, I love my native Lee,
　And its shamrock-spangled sod;
While I unfettered here can roam,
O, lure me not to your fairy home."

"Ha! free young chief, it will not be long,
　Ere freedom leaves your shore,
And these hills that echoed the patriots' song,
　Shall echo those strains no more;
When the Saxon churl, with lying tongue,
Has over your island his fetters flung."

"O, tempt me not, my place is here,
   If danger is so nigh;
Far better meet a bloody bier,
   Than like a coward fly;
For I will not sheathe my father's brand
While a Saxon lives to curse the land!"

The Fairy flung her harp aside,
   And gazed on him with grief;
And stepped upon the rippling tide,
   Beside the youthful chief;
And crouched within a glowing shell,
And slowly sank as she cried, farewell!

The young chief sat on the moss-clad stone,
   And pondered the fairy's words;
'Till he heard a Saxon trumpet blown,
   And the clang of Saxon swords.
And a crimson flush is on his brow,
For a score to one is around him now.

No mercy from the foe he sought—
   But wild his proud eyes gleam,
And gallantly the chieftain fought,
   Like a flashing lightning beam;
But he fell at length, without a groan,
And his red blood dyed the moss-clad stone.

The fairy came to the spot again,
   When the moon came o'er the hills;
And her sorrow for the hero slain,
   The dew-clad valley fills;
As she stooped beside the silent flood,
And kissed the stone dyed with his blood.

His clansmen laid him in the dell,
   Where branches o'er him quiver;
Beside the spot he loved so well,
   The ever-sparkling river;
Where oft the fairy queen has sighed,
Above the stone on which he died.

And time rolled over swift and fast,
   On rock and tree and flower;
And the moss-clad stone was built at last,
   In Blarney Castle tower
And they who kiss it, old or young,
Are gifted with the Fairy Tongue.

WISHES AND WISHES.
Francis Davis.[*]

Oh! know ye the wish of the true, the true!
Oh! know ye the wish of the true;
       'Tis to see the slave's hand,
       Whirling liberty's brand,
As its toil-nurtured muscles could do,
And the wide-world's oppressors in view:
God ripen the wish of the true!

Then hurrah for the wish of the true, the true!
Hurrah for the wish of the true;
       And another hurrah
       For the fast coming day,
When the many shall preach to the few,
From a gospel as pure as the dew—
Oh! there's hope in that wish of the true!

[*] Of Belfast.

Oh! know ye the wish of the proud, the proud!
Oh! know ye the wish of the proud;
    'Tis to empty their veins,
    'Mid the crashing of chains,
Ay, the veins of their heart, if allowed,
So the neck of oppression be bound,
What a holy wish that of the proud!

Then hurrah for the wish of the brave, the brave!
Hurrah for the wish of the brave,
    And hurrah for the band,
    And the casque-cleaving brand,
That the rights of a nation can save,
Or redeem by its world-lightening wave—
Heaven bless the broad brand of the brave!

THE WIDOW'S MESSAGE TO HER SON.
Ellen Forrester.[*]

"Remember, Denis, all I bade you say;
 Tell him we're well and happy, thank the Lord,
But of our troubles, since he went away,
 You'll mind, avick, and never say a word;
  Of cares and troubles, sure, we've all our share,
  The finest summer isn't always fair.

"Tell him the spotted heifer calved in May:
 She died, poor thing; but that you needn't mind;
Nor how the constant rain destroyed the hay;
 But tell him God to us was ever kind,
  And when the fever spread the country o'er,
  His mercy kept the 'sickness' from our door.

[*] Of the County Monaghan—now resident in Manchester; author of "Simple Strains," (Henderson, London.)

"Be sure you tell him how the neighbours came
  And cut the corn and stored it in the barn;
'Twould be as well to mention them by name—
  Pat Murphy, Ned M'Cabe and James M'Carn,
    And big Tim Daly from behind the hill;
  But say, agra—Oh, say I missed him still.

"They came with ready hands our toil to share—
  'Twas then I missed him most—my own right hand;
I felt, although kind hearts were around me there,
  The kindest heart beat in a foreign land.
    Strong hand! brave heart! oh severed far from me
  By many a weary league of shore and sea.

"And tell him she was with us—he'll know who:
  Mavourneen, hasn't she the winsome eyes,
The darkest, deepest, brightest, bonniest blue,
  I ever saw except in summer skies.
    And such black hair! it is the blackest hair
  That ever rippled o'er neck so fair.

"Tell him old Pincher fretted many a day,
  And moped, poor dog, 'twas well he didn't die,
Crouched by the road side how he watched the way,
  And sniffed the travellers as they passed him by—
    Hail, rain, or sunshine, sure, 'twas all the same,
  He listened for the foot that never came.

"Tell him the house is lonesome-like and cold,
  The fire itself seems robbed of half its light;
But, maybe, 'tis my eyes are growing old,
  And things look dim before my failing sight.
    For all that, tell him 'twas myself that spun
  The shirts you bring, and stitched them every one.

"Give him my blessing, morning, noon, and night,
  Tell him my prayers are offered for his good,
That he may keep his Maker still in sight,
  And firmly stand, as his brave father stood,
    True to his name, his country, and his God,
    Faithful at home, and steadfast still abroad."

THE APOSTLE'S GRAVE.
John Fitzgerald.*

The autumn winds went howling past,
The sere leaf rustled in the blast,
The thick dull rain fell pattering slow
On the quiet homes of the dead below.
My heart was sad as I raised my eye,
To the hurrying clouds in the dull grey sky;
And the cypress trees did sadly wave,
As I knelt beside the Apostle's grave.

I thought what a shadow was earthly fame,
And what was the use of an honoured name;
That he who sleeps 'neath that cold wet stone,
Had toiled unaided and struggled alone,
And Erinn freed from the iron thrall
Of the damning arch-fiend Alcohol;
And all he had gained in the land of his birth,
Was that simple cross and six feet of earth.

I looked, and away the dark clouds rolled,
And the sun looked out through banks of gold,
And the rainbow spanned the sparkling sod
Like the jewelled gate of the house of God;

* Author of the legendary ballad of "The Blarney Stone." A tradesman of Cork city.

And from the old stone cross* I heard
The joyous song of that sacred bird,†
Who reddened his breast against the bleeding side
Of Him who on that cross had died.
The prayers of the poor and the tears they shed,
Are the honours paid o'er his humble bed.

DRIMIN DONN DILIS.‡

JOHN WALSH.§

Oh! Drimin donn dilis! the landlord has come,
Like a foul blast of death has he swept o'er our home.
He has withered our rooftree—beneath the cold sky,
Poor, houseless and homeless, to-night must we lie.

---

* A simple stone cross, of massive proportions, without ornament of any kind, was erected by Father Mathew himself, in the cemetery which he established in Cork, and under this, at his own desire, his remains are interred. Overshadowing it grows a cedar of Lebanon, and close to it are always to be seen some of the poor at prayer. † The Robin.

‡ "*Drimin*" is the favourite name of a cow in the Gaelic tongue. In "The Ballad Poetry of Ireland." published by James Duffy, Dublin, and edited by Charles Gavan Duffy, there is given a translation by J. J. Callanan, of Cork, of a popular Irish Jacobite song; spirited and highly characteristic of the country. "Drimin" is also one of the allegorical names which the people applied to Ireland, by which they sheltered their expressions of love for their country, when it was a crime to praise her. There are in the country many fairy-tales connected with dark cows: the dark

---

§ Of Cappoquin, a town on the Blackwater, between Lismore and Cork.

My heart it is cold as the white winter's snow;
My brain is on fire, and my blood's in a glow.
Oh! Drimin donn dilis, 'tis hard to forgive
When a robber denies us the right we should live.

With my health and my strength, with hard labour and toil,
I dried the wet marsh and I tilled the harsh soil—
I moiled the long day through, from morn till even,
And I thought in my heart I'd a foretaste of Heaven.

The summer shone round us, above and below,
The beautiful summer that makes the flowers blow.
Oh! 'tis hard to forget it, and think I must bear
That strangers shall reap the reward of my care.

Your limbs they were plump then—your coat it was silk,
And never was wanted the mother of milk,
For freely it came in the calm summer's noon,
While you munched to the time of the old milking croon.

How often you left the green side of the hill,
To stretch in the shade and to drink of the rill;
And often I freed you before the grey dawn,
From your snug little pen at the edge of the bawn.

small breed of cows, which prevailed in the country, have a weird-like look about them. Owenson, father of Lady Morgan, used to sing on the Irish stage the old song, "Drimin Dhown Dheelish, thou silk of the kine," with such feeling as to bring tears to the eyes of all listeners who had any sympathy for their country. "Dhown" means "brown," and "dheelish" is a term expressive of the fondest affection.

But they racked and they ground me with tax and
  with rent, [spent;
'Till my heart it was sore, and my life-blood was
To-day they have finished; and on the wide world,
With the mocking of friends from my home was I
  hurled.

I knelt down three times for to utter a prayer,
But my heart it was seared, and the words were
  not there; [head came,
Oh! wild were the thoughts through my dizzy
Like the rushing of wind through a forest of flame.

I bid you, old comrade, a long last farewell,
For the gaunt hand of famine has clutched us too
  well;
It severed the master and you my good cow,
With a blight on his life, and a brand on his brow.

THE IRISH-AMERICAN.

Timothy D. Sullivan.[*]

Columbia, the free, is the land of my birth,
And my paths have been all on American earth;
But my blood is as Irish as any can be,
And my heart is with Erin afar o'er the sea.

My father and mother, and friends all around,
Are daughters and sons of the sainted old ground—
They rambled its bright plains and mountains among,
And filled its fair valleys with laugh and with song.

[*] Of "The Nation" newspaper. Author of a little volume entitled "Dunboy and other Poems."

But I sing their sweet music, and often they own
It is true to old Ireland in style and in tone;
I dance their gay dances, and hear them with glee,
Say each touch tells of Erin afar o'er the sea.

I have tufts of green shamrock in sods they brought o'er,
I have shells they picked up ere they stepped from the shore,
I have books that are treasures; the fondest I hold
Is "The Melodies," clasped and nigh covered with gold.

My pictures are pictures of scenes that are dear
For the beauties they are, or the glories they were,
And of good men and great men whose merits shall be
Long the pride of green Erin afar o'er the sea.

If I were in beautiful Dublin to-day,
To the spots I hold sacred I'd soon find my way,
For I know where O'Connell and Curran are laid,
And where loved Robert Emmett sleeps cold "in the shade."

And if I were in Wexford—how fondly I'd trace
Each field I have marked on my maps of the place,
Where the brave Ninety-Eight men poured hotly and free
Their blood for dear Erin afar o'er the sea.

Dear home of my fathers! I'd hold thee to blame,
And my cheeks would at times take the crimson of shame,   [line,
Did thy sad tale not show, in each sorrow-stained
That the might of thy tyrant was greater than thine.

But her soldiers are many, abroad and at home,
Her ships on all oceans are ploughing the foam,
And her wealth is untold—sure no equal was she,
For my poor plundered Erin afar o'er the sea.

Yet they tell me the strife is not yet given o'er—
That the gallant old Island will try it once more;
And will call, with her harp, when her flag is unfurled,
Her sons, and *their* sons, from the ends of the world.

If so, I've a heart never shaken with fear :
A brain that can plan, and a hand that can dare ;
And the summons will scarce have died out when
    I'll be,
'Mid the green fields of Erin afar o'er the sea.

THE RAPPAREE'S HORSE AND SWORD.
Robert Dwyer Joyce.

My name is Mac Sheehy, from Feal's swelling flood,
A Rapparee rover by mountain and wood,
I've two trusty comrades to serve me at need,
This sword by my side and my gallant grey steed.

Now where did I get them, my gallant grey steed
And this sword true and trusty, to serve me at
    need?
This sword was my father's—in battle he died—
And I reared bold Osgur by Feal's woody side!

I've said it, and say it, and care not who hear,
Myself and grey Osgur have never known fear—
There's a dint in my helmet, a hole through his ear,
'Twas the same bullet made them at Limerick last
    year!

And the soldier who fired it was still ramming down,
When this long sword came right with a slash on
　his crown—
Dar Dia! but he'll never fire musket again,
For his skull lies in two at the side of the glen!

When they caught us one day at the castle of
　Brugh,
Of our black-hearted foemen the deadliest crew,
Like a bolt from the thunder grey Osgur went
　through,
And my sword! long they'll weep at the sore
　taste of you!

Together we sleep 'neath the wild crag or tree;
My soul, but there ne'er were such comrades as we!
I, Brian the Rover, my two friends at need,
This sword by my side and my gallant grey steed!

FISHERMAN'S PRAYER.
Timothy D. Sullivan.

The sun is setting angrily,
　In threat'ning gusts the wind is blowing,
Holy Mary! Star of the Sea!
Speed our small bark fast and free
　O'er the homeward way we're going!

We left the land as the morning bright
　Purpled the smooth sea all before us;
We prayed to God and our hearts were light,
We placed our bark in thy saving sight,
　And knew thou would'st well watch o'er us.

But now the sun sets angrily,
   From black wild clouds the wind is blowing,
Holy Mary! Star of the Sea!
Send our small bark fast and free
   O'er the darkling way we're going!

We fished the deep the live-long day,
   The waves were rich, through God's good pleasure;
We ventured far from our own bright bay,
And lingered late; we fain would stay,
   'Till filled with the shining treasure.

But now the night falls threat'ningly,
   The seas run high with the fierce wind blowing,
Holy Mary! Star of the Sea!
Our light, our guide, our safety be,
   O'er the stormy way we're going!

We pass the point where the tempest's strain
   Is lighten'd off by the land's high cover;
Our village lights shine out again—
I know my own in my window pane,
   And the tall church glooming over.

Holy Mary! Star of the Sea!
   With grateful love our hearts are glowing;
Behold we bless Thy Son and thee!
Oh, still our light and safety be
   O'er the last dread course we're going!

THE CAILIN DEAS.

Air—"Cailín beaſ cṅúiṫce na m-bó!"

The gold rain of eve was descending,
  Bright purple robed mountain and tree,
As I through Glenmornein was wending,
  A wanderer from o'er the blue sea.
'Twas the lap of a West-looking mountain,
  Its woody slope bright with the glow,
Where sang by a murmuring fountain,
  An cailín beaſ cṅúiṫce na m-bó.

Dark clouds where a gold tinge reposes
  But picture her brown, wavy hair,
And her teeth look'd as if, in a rose's
  Red bosom a snow-flake gleamed fair.
As her tones down the green dell went ringing,
  The list'ning thrush mimicked them low,
And the brooklet harped soft to the singing
  Of cailín beaſ cṅúiṫce na m-bó.

"At last, o'er thy long night, dear Erin!
  Dawns the Sun of thy Freedom," sang she;
"But thy mountaineers still are despairing—
  Ah, he who mid bondmen was free,
Ah, my Diarmid, the Patriot-hearted,
  Who would fire them with hope for the blow,
Far, Erin! from thee is he parted,
  Far from cailín beaſ cṅúiṫce na m-bó."

* "An cailin deas cruidte na m-bo," should be pronounced by the mere English reader as "collyeen dass crootia na mo"—it signifies, "The pretty girl of the milking of cows," or the pretty milkmaid.

Her tears on a sudden, brimmed over,
  Her voice trembled low and less clear;
To listen, I stepped from my cover,
  But the bough-rustle broke on her ear;
She started—she redden'd—" A Stoirin !*
  My Diarmid !—Oh, *can* it be so ?"
And I clasped to my glad heart sweet Moirin,
  Ꮎo cᴀɪʟɪɴ ᴅᴇᴀʀ cʀúɪᴏᴛᴇ ɴᴀ m-ʙó !

OWEN REILLY: A KEEN.
(From the Irish.)
CLARENCE MANGAN.—TRANSLATOR.

Oh ! lay aside the flax, and put away the wheel,
  And sing with me, but not in gladness—
The heart that's in my breast is like to break with
    sadness—
  God, God alone knows what I feel !

There's a lone, a vacant place beside the cheerless
    hearth,
  A spot my eyes are straining after—
Oh ! never more from thence will ring my boy's
    light laughter,
  The out-gushing of his young heart's mirth !

No more will his hands clasp the cross before the
    shrine
  Of Christ's immaculate Virgin Mother !
Never, oh ! never more will he pour forth another
  Prayer for himself, or me, or mine !

* " Vulgo, Asthoreen."

The young men on the mountain sides will miss—
    miss long,
  The fleetest hurler of their number
Powerless, alas! to-night in death's unbroken
    slumber,
  Lies he, the Lithe of Limb, the Strong!

Oh! raise the keen, young women, o'er my darling's
    grave—
  Oh! kneel in prayer o'er his low dwelling;
At break of day this morn there knelt his mother
    telling
  Her beads for him she could not save!

Oh! plant, young men, the shamrock near my
    darling's head,
  And raise the hardy fir-tree over
The spot: the strange way-fayer then will know
    they cover
  My Oweneen's dark burial-bed!

Heard ye not, yestreen, the banshee deplore
  His death on heath-clad Killinvallen?
"Ul-ullalu!" she cried, "a green young oak is
    fallen,
  For Owen Reilly lives no more!"

There stands a lone grey hazel-tree in Glen-na-ree
  Whose green leaves but bud forth and wither—
I sigh and groan as often as I wander thither,
  For I am like that lone grey tree!

My four beloved sons, where are they? have they not
  Left me a wreck here all as lonely?
They withered and they died! I, their old mother,
  Remain to weep and wail their lot!

But I will follow them now soon; for oft amid
    The storm I hear their voices calling,
"Come home!"—and in my dreams I see the
    cold clay falling
    Heavily on my coffin-lid!
When the dark night films o'er my eyes, oh! let
    me be
    Laid out by Aileen Bawn Devany;
And let the lights around me at my wake be as
    many
    As the white hairs yet left to me!

See that the tall white slender gowans blow and
    bloom
    In the grass round my headstone brightly;
I would not have the little orphan-daisy nightly
    Mourning in solitude and gloom!

Let there be shrieking on the hill and in the glen,
    Throughout the length and breadth of Galway's
Green land! where Kathleen Dubh Reilly has her-
    self been always
    The Queen of Keeners: mourn her, then!

Lights will be seen to dance along Carn Corra's
    height,
    And through the burial-field; but follow
Them not, young men and women! for, o'er hill
    and hollow,
    They will but lure to Death and Night!

But, come ye to my grave when, in the days of May,
    The gladsome sun and skies grow warmer,
And say, "Here sleeps Kathleen, where tempest
    cannot harm her,
    Soft be her narrow bed of clay!"

And count your beads, and pray, " Rest her poor
    soul, oh, God!
  She willed no ill to breathing mortal—
Grant her then, Thou, a place within Heaven's
    blessed portal,
  Now that her bones lie in the sod!"

FINEEN THE ROVER.
ROBERT DWYER JOYCE.
AIR—"You'd think, if you heard their pipes squealing."

An old castle towers o'er the billow
  That thunders by Cleena's green land,
And there dwelt as gallant a rover
  As ever grasped hilt by the hand—
Eight stately towers of the waters
  Lie anchored in Baltimore Bay,
And over their twenty score sailors,
  Oh, who but the Rover holds sway?
    Then ho! for Fineen the rover!
    Fineen O'Driscoll the free!
    Straight as the mast of his galley,
    And wild as the wave of the sea!

The Saxons of Cork and Moyallo,
  They harried his lands with their powers;
He gave them a taste of his cannon,
  And drove them like wolves from his towers.
The men of Clan London brought over
  Their strong fleet to make him a slave;
They met him by Mizen's wild highland,
  And the sharks crunched their bones 'neath the
    wave!

>   Then ho! for Fineen the Rover,
>   Fineen O'Driscoll the free,
>   With step like the red stag of Beara,
>   And voice like the bold sounding sea.

Long time in that old battered castle,
   Or out on the waves with his clan
He feasted, and ventured, and conquered,
   But ne'er struck his colours to man.
In a fight 'gainst the foes of his country,
   He died as a brave man should die,
And he sleeps 'neath the waters of Cleena,
   Where the waves sing his *caoine* to the sky!
>   Then ho! for Fineen the Rover,
>   Fineen O'Driscoll the free,
>   With eye like the Osprey's at morning,
>   And smile like the sun on the sea.

THE NEW RACE.
Aubrey De Vere.

O ye who have vanquished the land and retain it,
   How little ye know what ye miss of delight!
There are worlds in her heart—could ye seek it or gain it—
   That would clothe a true noble with glory and might.
What is she, this isle which ye trample and ravage,
   Which ye plough with oppression and reap with the sword,
But a harp never strung in the hall of a savage,
   Or a fair wife embraced by a husband abhorred?

The chiefs of the Gael were the people embodied !
    The chiefs were the blossoms, the people the root ;
Their conquerors, the Normans, high-souled and
        high-blooded,
    Grew Irish at last from the scalp to the foot.
And ye !—ye are hirelings and satraps, not nobles !
    Your slaves, they detest you ; your masters they
        scorn !
The river lives on—but the sun-painted bubbles
    Pass quick, to the rapids incessantly borne.

THE LULLABY.
OWEN ROE O'SULLIVAN.*
EDWARD WALSH†—TRANSLATOR.

Hush, baby mine, and weep no more ;
Each gem thy regal fathers wore,
When Erinn, Emerald Isle, was free,
Thy poet-sire bequeathes to thee !
    Hush, baby dear, and weep no more !
    Hush, baby mine, my treasured store ;
    My heart-wrung sigh, my grief, my groan,
    Thy tearful eye, thy hunger's moan !

The steed of golden housings rare,
Bestowed by glorious Falvey Fair
The chief who at the Boyne did shroud
In bloody wave, the sea-kings proud !
    Hush, baby dear.

    * His extempore effusion: to soothe the sorrows of his child—the mother being absent.
    † Died at Cork in 1850. About seven years after his demise a few of the working men of Cork, raised in the Mathew cemetery, a graceful monument to his memory.

Brian's golden-hilted sword of light,
That flashed despair on foeman's flight ;
And Murcha's fierce, far-shooting bow,
That at Clontarf laid heroes low !
    Hush, baby dear.

The courier hound that tidings bore
From Cashel to Bunratty's shore ;
An eagle fierce, a bird of song,
And Skellig's hawk, the fierce and strong.
    Hush, baby dear.

Fingal's swift sword of death and fear,
And Dearmid's host-compelling spear ;
The helm that guarded Oscar's head
When fierce Mac Treon beneath him bled.
    Hush, baby dear.

Son of old chiefs ! to thee is due
The gift Aoife gave her champions true,
That sealed for aye Ferdia's doom,
And gave young Conlaoch to the tomb.
    Hush, baby dear

Nor shall it be ungiven unsung,
The mantle dark of Dulaing young,
That viewless left the chief who laid
Whole hosts beneath his battle-blade !
    Hush, baby dear.

Another boon shall grace thy hand,
Mac Duivne's life-protecting brand,
Great Aongus' gift, when Fenian foe
Pursued his path with shaft and bow !
    Hush, baby dear.

And dainty rich, and beoir* I'll bring,
And raiment meet for chief and king ;
But gift and song shall yield to joy—
Thy mother comes to greet her boy !
   Hush, baby dear, and weep no more,
   Hush, baby mine, my treasured store,
   My heart-wrung sigh, my grief, my groan,
   Thy tearful eye, thy hunger's moan !

SLIAV-NA-MAN.

A Ballad of 'Ninety-Eight,

(From the Irish.)

George Sigerson, Translator.

Air—" Not more welcome the fairy numbers."

Weep the great Departed—the Patriot-hearted !
   With life they parted for Ireland's right ;
To them give glory, while tyrants gory
   Spread the false story, " they fled in fright."
O, 'twas small our terror ! we fell to Error,
   No chiefs there were or an ordered van ;
Yet when came war's rattle we fled not battle,
   Though like herdless cattle on Sliav-na-Man !

May the grief each ray shuns curse their impatience,
   Who did haste our Nation's uprise from night,
Ere the South could gather its clanns together,
   And on this heather with the West unite.

  * A liquor, anciently made from mountain-heath.

Our camp had warriors!—Ay, Freedom's barriers!
  The God-sent carriers of Slav'ry's van!
O, no spy had found them—no fetter bound them,
  We'd be freed men round them on Sliav-na-man.

Though at Ross defeated, few, few retreated;
  Death comes—they meet it with push of pike!
Then were dragged the *dying*, and poor babes crying,
  The flames to lie in, from ditch and dyke;
Ye who wreaked this slaughter, for the crimes you wrought there
  We swear—like water your blood shall run,
Yet—savage yeomen, of Hell an omen,
  We'll meet ye, foemen, on Sliav-na-man!

Ah! many old man and star-bright bold man,
  Who long did hold on to free their Isle,
Lie pale and markless, in deathy starkness,
  Bowed down in darkness of dungeon vile.
There, eve and morning, they bear all scorning,
  Threats, lashes, mourning, that their tyrants plan;
We'll pay, soon, your labours, O coward neighbours!
  With our trusty sabres on Sliav-na-man!

For on the Ocean are ships in motion,
  And glad devotion on France's shore,
And rumour's telling; "they'll now be sailing
  To help the Gael in the Right once more."
O! if true's that story, by my hopes of glory,
  Like the glad bird o'er me I'll lilt my rann!
Were the robber routed! the Saxon flouted!
  How we would shout it, old Sliav-na-man!

Ho! the clowns are quaking and counsel taking,
　Good times are making their firm approach,
When those who weakly still preach "bear meekly,"
　Will mourn all bleakly in dark reproach!
While gold and chattel, broad lands and cattle
　Pay them whose battle made freedom dawn,
And way-side dances our joy enhances,
　With the gold fire-glances o'er Sliav-na-man!

MAC KENNA'S DREAM.*
STREET BALLAD.

One night of late I chanced to stray,
When all the Green in slumber lay,
　　The moon sunk in the deep;
I sat upon a ruined mound
And while the wild wind whistled round,
The ocean with a solemn sound
　　Lulled me fast asleep.

I dreamt I saw that hero true,
Who did the Danish force subdue;
His sabre bright, with wrath he drew,
　　These words he said to me;

---

* This ballad seems an especial favourite with "the common people."—In every handful of Street Ballad Slips, whether printed in Belfast, Dublin, or Cork, I have found this turning up—I have abridged the ballad, as the rustic author seems to have indulged his love of rhyming, and of summoning the Great Departed to his mind's eye, to an extent that might tire the patience of my readers.

"The Harp, with rapture, yet shall sound,
My children's chains shall be unbound,
And they shall gather safe around
  The blooming laurel tree."

I thought brave Sarsfield drew up nigh,
And to my question made reply;
"For Erinn's cause I'll live and die
  As thousands did before.
My sword again on Aughrim's plain
Old Erinn's rights shall well maintain,
Through millions in the battle slain
  And thousands in their gore."

I thought Saint Ruth stood on the ground
And said, "I'll be your monarch crowned,
Encompassed by the French around
  All marching to the field;
He raised a Cross, and thus did say,
"Brave boys, we'll show them gallant play;
Let no man dare disgrace the day,
  We'll die before we yield."

The brave O'Byrne he was there,
From Ballymanus, bright and fair,
Brought Wicklow, Carlow and Kildare,
  To march at his command:
Westmeath and Cavan too did join,
The county Louth men crossed the Boyne,
Slane, Trim, and Navan too did join
  With Dublin to a man.

O'Reilly, on the hill of Screene,
He drew his sword, both bright and keen,
And swore by all his eyes had seen,
  He would avenge the fall

Of Erinn's sons and daughters brave,
Who nobly filled a martyr's grave,
And died, rather than live a slave,
    And still for vengeance call.

Then Father Murphy came to say,
" Behold, my lord, I'm here to-day,
With eighteen thousand pikemen gay,
    From Wexford's hills and caves :
Our country's fate, it sure depends
On us, and on our gallant friends,
And heaven will their cause defend,
    Who ne'er were willing slaves."

I thought the band played " Patrick's Day "
To marshal all in grand array ;
With cap and feather, white and gay
    They marched in warlike glow,
With drums and trumpets loud and shrill,
And cannon upon every hill,
And pike-men, who, with valour thrill
    To strike the fatal blow.

When all at once, appeared in sight
An army clad in armour bright,
Both front, and rere, and left, and right
    Marched Puddies evermore.
The chieftains pitched their camps with skill,
Determined tyrants' blood to spill,
Beneath us ran a mountain rill,
    As rapid as the Nore.

A Frenchman brave rose up and said,
" Let Erinn's sons be not dismayed,
To glory I'll the vanguard lead,
    To honour and renown.

Come, bravely draw your swords with me,
And let each tyrant bigot see
Dear Erinn's daughters must be free
    Before the sun goes down.

Along the line they raised a shout
Crying " Quick march, right about ;"
With bayonets fixed they all marched out
    To face the deadly foe.
The enemy were no-ways shy
With thundering cannon planted nigh;
Now thousands in death-struggle lie,
    And streams of crimson flow.

The enemy made such a square
As drove our cavalry to despair
Who were nigh routed, rank, and rere,
    But yet not forced to yield.
The Wexford boys that ne'er were slack,
Came, with the brave Tips at their back,
With Longford joined, who in a crack,
    Soon sent them off the field.

They gave three cheers for Liberty,
As the enemy all broken flee ;
I looked around, but could not see
    One foeman on the plain,
Except the men who wounded lay :
When I awoke 'twas break of day—
    So ends MacKenna's dream.

BROSNA'S BANKS
J. FRAZER.*

Yes, yes, I idled many an hour—
    Oh! would that I could idle now,
In wooing back the withered flower
    Of health into my wasted brow!
But from my life's o'ershadowing close,
    My unimpassioned spirit ranks
Among its happiest moments those
    I idled on the Brosna's Banks.

For there upon my boyhood broke
    The dreamy voice of nature first;
And every word that vision spoke,
    How deeply has my spirit nursed!
A woman's love, a lyre, or pen,
    A rescued land, a nation's thanks,
A friendship with the world, and then
    A grave upon the Brosna's Banks.

For these I sued, and sought, and strove:
    But now my youthful days are gone,
In vain, in vain,—for woman's love
    Is still a blessing to be won;
And still my country's cheek is wet,
    The still unbroken fetter clanks,
And I may not forsake her yet
    To die upon the Brosna's Banks.

---

* Died in Dublin in 1849. A cabinet maker—a steady and unassuming workman; author of a volume of patriotic verse. Was born on the banks of the Brosna, in the King's county.

Yet idle as those visions seem,
    They were a strange and faithful guide,
When Heaven itself had scarce a gleam
    To light my darkened life beside;
And if from grosser guilt escaped,
    I feel no dying dread, the thanks
Are due unto the power that shaped
    My visions on the Brosna's Banks.

And love, I feel, will come at last,
    Albeit too late to comfort me;
And fetters from the land be cast,
    Though I may not survive to see.
If then the gifted, good, and brave,
    Admit me to their glorious ranks,
My memory may, though not my grave,
    Be green upon the Brosna's Banks.

THE BARD ETHELL.
Thirteenth Century.
AUBREY DE VERE.

[The Bard Ethell, now blind and old, son of Conn, and Clansman to Brian, having told who he is, where he dwells, and how he lives, proceeds to tell of King Malachi.]

There never was King, and never will be
In battle or banquet like Malachi!
The Seers his reign had predicted long;
He honoured the bards, and gave gold for song.
If rebels arose he put out their eyes;
    If robbers plundered or burned the fanes,
He hung them in chaplets, like rosaries,
    That others beholding might take more pains!

There was none to women more reverent-minded,
    For he held his mother, and Mary, dear;
If any man wronged them, that man he blinded,
    Or straight amerced him of hand or ear.
There was none who founded more convents—none;
    In his palace the old and poor were fed;
The orphan might walk, or the widow's son,
    Without groom or page to his throne or bed.
In his council he mused, with great brows divine,
And eyes like the eyes of the musing kine,
Upholding a sceptre whereon their sate,
With her wings o'er empires, a sleep-tranced Fate.
He drained ten lakes and he built ten bridges;
    He bought a gold book for a thousand cows;
He slew ten princes who brake their pledges;
    With the bribed and the base he scorned to carouse.
He was sweet and awful; through all his reign
God gave great harvests to vale and plain:
From his nurse's milk he was kind and brave:
And when he went down to his well-wept grave,
Through the triumph of penance his soul uprose
To God and the Saints. Not so his foes!

[The Bard Ethell's account of the King who succeeded Malachi.].

The King who came after! ah, woe, woe, woe!
He doubted his friend and trusted his foe.
He bought and he sold: his kingdom old
    He pledged and he pawned to avenge a spite:
No bard or prophet his birth foretold:
    He was guarded and warded both day and night:

He counselled with fools and bad boors at his feast;
He was cruel to Christian and kind to beast:
Men smiled when they talked of him far o'er the
    wave :
Well paid were the mourners who wept o'er his
    grave.
God plagued for his sake his people sore :—
    They sinned ; for the people should watch and
        pray
That their prayers, like angels at window and door,
    May keep from the king the bad thoughts away !

[The Bard Ethell's picture of Norna ; a young girl
to whom he had been an instructor.]

The sun has risen : on lip and brow
    He greets me—I feel it—with golden wand.
Ah, bright-faced Norna! I see thee now—
    Where first I saw thee I see thee stand !
From the trellis the girl looked down on me :
Her maidens stood near :—it was late in spring :
The grey priest laughed as she cried in glee,
    "Good bard, a song in my honour sing."
I sang her praise in a loud-voiced hymn
To God who had fashioned her, face and limb,
For the praise of the clan and the land's behoof:
So she flung me a flower from the trellis roof.
Ere long I saw her the hill descending—
    O'er the lake the May morning rose moist and slow :
She prayed me (her smile with the sweet voice
        blending)
    To teach her all that a woman should know.

Panting she stood : she was out of breath :
   The wave of her little breast was shaking :
From eyes still childish and dark as death
Came womanhood's dawn through a dew-cloud
   breaking.
Norna was never long time the same :
   By a spirit so strong was her slight form moulded
The curves swelled out of the flower-like frame
   In joy ; in grief to a bud she folded :
As she listened her eyes grew bright and large
Like springs rain-fed that dilate their marge.

[The Bard Ethell's instruction of Norna.]

So I taught her the hymn of Patrick the Apostle,
   And the marvels of Briget and Columbkille :
And ere long she sang like the lark or the throstle,
   Sang the deeds of the servants of God's high will :
I told her of Brendon who found afar
Another world 'neath the western star ;
Of our three great bishops in Lindisfarne isle ;
Of St. Fursey the wond'rous, Fiacre without guile ;
Of Scotus the subtle who clove a hair
Into sixty parts, and had marge to spare.
To her brother I spake of Oisin and Fionn,
And they wept at the death of great Oisin's son.
I taught the heart of the boy to revel
   In tales of old greatness that never tire,
And the virgin's, up-springing from earth's low level,
   To wed with heaven like the altar fire.
I taught her all that a woman should know :
   And that none should teach her worse lore, I
     gave her
A dagger keen, and taught her the blow
That subdues the knave to discreet behaviour.

A sand-stone there on my knee she sat,
And sharpened its point—I can see her yet—
I held back her hair and she sharpened the edge,
While the wind piped low through the reeds and
  sedge.

[The Bard Ethell again speaks of himself—of the Saxon rule which is reported to be spreading over Erinn; the truth of which rumour he doubts—and concludes thus;—]

Ah me, that man who is made of dust
  Should have pride towards God ! 'tis an Angel's
    sin !
I have often feared lest God, the All-just,
  Should bend from heaven and sweep earth clean,
Should sweep us all into corners and holes,
Like dust of the house-floor, both bodies and souls :—
I have often feared He would send some wind
In wrath ; and the nation wake up stone-blind !
In age or in youth we have all wrought ill :—
I say not our great King Niall did well
(Although he was Lord of the pledges nine)
  When, beside subduing this land of Eire,
He raised in Amorica banner and sign,
  And wasted the British coast with fire:
Perhaps in his mercy the Lord will say,
" These men, these men ? 'twas a rough boy-play !"
He is certain—that young Franciscan priest—
God sees great sins where men see least.
Yet this were to give unto God the eye
(Unmeet the thought) of the humming fly !
I trust there are small things he scorns to see
In the lowly who cry to him piteously.

Our hope is Christ.   I have wept full oft
   He came not to Eire in Oisin's time ;
Though love and those new monks, would make
    men soft
   If they were not hardened by war and rhyme.
I have done my part : my end draws nigh :
I shall leave old Eire with a smile and sigh :
She will miss not me as I missed my son :
Yet for her, and her praise, were my best deeds
    done.
Man's deeds! Man's deeds ; they are shades that
    fleet,
Or ripples like those that break at my feet.
The deeds of my chief and the deeds of my king
Grow hazy, far seen, in the hills in spring.
Nothing is great save the death on the cross !
   But Pilate and Herod I hate, and know
   Had Fionn lived then he had laid them low,
Though the world thereby had sustained great loss.
My blindness and deafness and aching back
With meekness I bear for that sufferer's sake ;
And the lent-fast for Mary's sake I love,
And the honour of Him, the Man Above !
My songs are all over now :—so best!
They are laid in the heavenly Singer's breast,
Who never sings but a star is born :
May we hear His song in the endless morn !
I give glory to God for our battles won
   By wood or river, on bay or creek :
For Norna, who died ; for my father, Conn :
   For feasts, and the chase on the mountains bleak :
I bewail my sins, both unknown and known,
   And of those I have injured forgiveness seek.

The men that were wicked to me and mine;
(Not quenching a wrong, nor in war nor wine),
I forgive and absolve them all, save three :*—
May Christ in His mercy be kind to me!

BLARNEY GROVES.

J. L. Forest.†

Oh! I could linger out a summer day
   Beneath thy groves, sweet Blarney; by thy lake,
   Thy meads, thy streams, and every flowery brake
For hours delighted, I could gladly stray,
   And breathe the fragrance of the perfumed air.
Wild flowers begem each wooded, shaded way,
   And modestly their trembling petals rear;
   To me than rich exotics far more fair,
And graceful-like. Ye seek the sun-light's ray
   In bashfulness, from tangled briars peeping,
   Or timidly amidst the long grass creeping,
But always winning in the garb ye wear.
Children of nature, fitly do ye play
   Beneath the ruined walls of yon old ruin grey;

---

* In an earlier portion of his poem he says :—
  "*I* forgive old Cathbar who sank my boat;
   Must I pardon Feargal who slew my son ;—
  Or the pirate, Strongbow, who burned Granote,
   They tell me, and in it nine priests, a nun,
  And (worst) St. Finian's old crosier staff.
  At forgiveness like that I spit and laugh !'

† Of Cork—died recently in America.

Relic of time! his heavy hand had leant
  Too hardly on thee; yet withal thou hast
  Around thee still fine traces of the Past,
The glorious Past, in every lineament.
  Type of my country! Strength and ruin blent—
Thou standest forth, amid the thunder-shower,
  A thing of grandeur; storm on storm hath spent
Its rage upon thee, yet round yon old tower
  The ivy twines its tendrils through each rent.
Thus ERINN, thou, 'mid Desolation's blast,
'Mid crushing storms and blighted hopes dost wear
  Perennial green! unlike yon mouldering pile,
Thy day of glory dawns, when thou shalt bear
  A form of life, and bask in Freedom's blessed smile!

THE CLADDAGH BOATMAN.

JEREMIAH J. DOWLING.*

I am a Claddagh boatman bold,
  And humble is my calling,
From morn to night, from dark to light,
  In Galway bay I'm trawling;
I care not for the great man's frown,
  I ask not for his pity;
My wants are few, my heart is true,
  I sing a boatman's ditty.

I have a fair and gentle wife,
  Her name is Eily Holway;
With many a wile, and joke, and smile,
  I won the pride of Galway;

* Of Tipperary.

For twenty years, 'mid hopes and fears,
　　With her I've faithful tarried;
Her heart to-night is young and light,
　　As when we first were married.

I have a son, a gallant boy,
　　Unstained by spot or speckle:
He pulls and hawls, and mends the trawls,
　　And minds the other tackle;
His mother says, the boy, like me,
　　Loves truth and hates all blarney—
The neighbours swear, in Galway bay
　　There's not the like of Barney.

Thank God, I have another child,
　　Like Eily, lithe and slender;
She clasps my knee and kisses me
　　With love so true and tender.
'Though oft' will rage the howling blast
　　Upon the angry water,
I ne'er complain of wind or rain,
　　For I think of my little daughter.

When Sunday brings the hours of rest,
　　That sweet reward of labours,
We cross the fields to early mass
　　And walk home with the neighbours.
Oh! would the rest of Erinn's sons
　　Were but like us united;
To swear I'm loath, but by my oath,
　　Her name should not be slighted.

LOVE BALLAD.
(From the Irish.)
CLARENCE MANGAN.[*]

Lonely from my home I come,
  To cast myself upon your tomb,
        And to weep.
Lonely from my lonesome home,
  My lonesome house of grief and gloom,
        While I keep
Vigil, often all night long,
  For your dear, dear sake,
Praying many a prayer so wrong
  That my heart would break!

Gladly, O my blighted flower,
  Sweet Apple of my bosom's Tree,
        Would I now
Stretch me in your dark death-bower
  Beside your corpse, and lovingly
        Kiss your brow:
But we'll meet ere many a day,
  Never more to part,
For even now I feel the clay
  Gathering round my heart.

In my soul doth darkness dwell,
  And through its dreary winding caves
        Ever flows,
Ever flows with moaning swell,
  One ebbless flood of many Waves,
        Which are Woes.

---

[*] An interesting memoir of Mangan by John Mitchel, will be found prefixed to the American edition of Mangan's Poems.

Death, love, has me in his lures,
  But that grieves not me,
So my ghost may meet with your's
  On yon moon-loved lea.

When the neighbours near my cot
  Believe me sunk in slumber deep,
          I arise—
For, O! 'tis a weary lot,
  This watching aye, and wooing sleep
          With hot eyes—
I arise and seek your grave,
  And pour forth my tears;
While the winds that nightly rave,
  Whistle in mine ears.

Often turns my memory back
  To that dear evening in the dell,
         When we twain
Sheltered by the Sloe-bush black,
  Sat, laughed, and talked, while thick sleet fell,
         And cold rain.
Thanks to God! no guilty leaven
  Dashed our childish mirth.
You rejoice for this in Heaven,
  And I not less on earth!

Love! the priests feel wroth with me,
  To find I shrine your image still
         In my breast.
Since you are gone eternally,
  And your fair frame lies in the chill
         Grave at rest;

But true Love outlives the shroud,
    Knows not check nor change,
And beyond Time's world of Cloud
    Still must reign and range.

Well may now your kindred mourn
    The threats, the wiles, the cruel arts,
               They long tried
On the child they left forlorn!
    They broke the tenderest heart of hearts,
               And she died.
Curse upon the love of show!
    Curse on Pride and Greed!
They would wed you " high"—and woe!
    Here behold their meed!

REPOSE:

GLENGARIFF BAY.

Ralph Varian.

By grassy marge, where shadows float,
    In day-dreams of delight we lay;
While, on white wing, a fairy boat
    Scarce rippled the enchanted Bay.

The drooping mountains bathed within,
    In green and gold, their woodland breast,
And crimson clouds, on dappled wing,
    At sweet Glengariff stooped to rest.

The mountain heights beyond, leant back,
    On flood-lights of departing day,
And murmurs from the torrent's track
    Stole o'er the margin where we lay.

Light Odours, from the myrtle ground,
    Crept through the yew and holly slopes,
And, whispering with the flowers around,
    Of sweet Glengariff's glories spoke.

From fruitful groves, grey speckled throats
    Low whistle to the fading day ;
From far off heights, faint bugle-notes
    Are gliding o'er the silent Bay.

From entrance of the sheltered Bay
    The sea-fowl snowy radiance bring;
While, in the woods that stretch away,
    The cooing pigeons fold the wing.

We touch the waters of the Bay,
    And taste the Ocean's briny lip ;
And on the rocks that shelve away
    The purple sea-plants float and dip.

The giant head of Sliav-na-goil,
    Lord of the glorious lonely height,
Stoops to the call of Adragol,
    Soft splashy sounds of calm delight.

The path it fans that we had trod,
    Which human footsteps seldom pressed,
The timid flower and beaming sod,
    With rose, and amber-woodbine dressed.

At File-Chonnan the eagle nests,
    And feeds her callow young with prey ;
Her storm-strong plumage gently rests
    In clefts that face the sheltered Bay.

From north fair Remacen lowly slopes—
   That soft and pleasant headland there—
And fond desires, and glorious hopes
   Flow through the sunset flooded air.

Advancing o'er the head of Dehade
   The crescent star of evening stoops;
And, peering through the vaulted shade,
   Advance the constellated groups.

We toiled o'er Gougane's rugged height,
   And wild and lonely Keim-an-eigh;
And, Mary, here, where all is bright
   We rest beside this tranquil Bay.

We saw wild Kerry's wonders thrown
   In garniture of summer-day;
And thought not pastoral Cork could own
   These mountains, and this heavenly Bay.

With awe and wonder welling there,
   Yet breathless as the closing day,
Our hearts sent up a silent prayer
   For glories of Glengariff Bay!

THE SHAN VAN VOCHT.
Charles J. Kickham.

There are ships upon the sea,
      Says the Shan Van Vocht;
There are good ships on the sea,
      Says the Shan Van Vocht,

Oh they're sailing o'er the sea,
From a land where all are free,
With a freight that's dear to me,
    Says the Shan Van Vocht.

They are coming from the West,
    Says the Shan Van Vocht;
And the flag we love the best,
    Says the Shan Van Vocht,
Waves proudly in the blast,
And they've nailed it to the mast;
Long threat'ning comes at last,
    Says the Shan Van Vocht.

'Twas well O'Connell said—
    Says the Shan Van Vocht—
"My land, when I am dead"—
    Says the Shan Van Vocht,
"A race will tread your plains
With hot blood in their veins,
Who will burst your galling chains,"
    Says the Shan Van Vocht.

For these words we love his name,
    Says the Shan Van Vocht,
And Ireland guards his fame,
    Says the Shan Van Vocht,
And low her poor heart fell
The day she heard his knell,
For she knew he loved her well,
    Says the Shan Van Vocht.

But the good old cause was banned,
      Says the Shan Van Vocht,
By sleek slave and traitor bland,
      Says the Shan Van Vocht,
Ah, then strayed to foreign strand
Truth and Valour from our land,
The stout heart and ready hand,
      Says the Shan Van Vocht.

But with courage undismayed,
      Says the Shan Van Vocht,
These exiles watched and prayed—
      Says the Shan Van Vocht;
For, though trampled to the dust
Their cause they knew was just,
And in God they put their trust,
      Says the Shan Van Vocht.

And now, if ye be men,
      Says the Shan Van Vocht.
We'll have them back again—
      Says the Shan Van Vocht,
With pike and guns galore,
And when they touch her shore
Ireland's free for evermore—
      Says the Shan Van Vocht.

THE SHANNON.
Gerald Griffin.

'Tis, it is the Shannon's stream
  Brightly glancing, brightly glancing,
See, oh, see the ruddy beam
  Upon its waters dancing!

Thus returned from travel vain,
Years of exile, years of pain,
To see old Shannon's face again,
　Oh, the bliss entrancing!
Hail our own majestic stream,
　Flowing ever, flowing ever,
Silent in the morning beam,
　Our own beloved river!

Fling thy rocky portals wide,
　Western Ocean, western Ocean,
Bend, ye hills! on either side,
　In solemn, deep devotion;
While before the rising gales
On his heaving surface sails,
Half the wealth of Erinn's vales,
　With undulating motion.
Hail our own beloved stream,
　Flowing ever, flowing ever,
Silent in the morning beam;
　Our own majestic river!

On thy bosom deep and wide,
　Noble river, lordly river,
Royal navies safe might ride,
　Green Erinn's lovely river!
Proud upon thy banks to dwell,
Let me ring Ambition's knell,
'Lured by Hope's illusive spell
　Again to wander never.
Hail, our own romantic stream
　Flowing ever, flowing ever,
Silent in the morning beam,
　Our own majestic river!

Let me from thy placid course,
  Gentle river, mighty river,
Draw such truth of silent force
  As sophists answer never.
Thus, like thee, unchanging still,
With tranquil breast and ordered will,
My heaven-appointed course fulfil,
  Undeviating ever!
Hail, our own majestic stream,
  Flowing ever, flowing ever,
Silent in the morning beam,
  Our own delightful river!

THE DRINAN DONN.*
ROBERT DWYER JOYCE.

By road and by river the wild birds sing,
O'er mountain and valley the dewy leaves spring,
The gay flowers are shining, gilt o'er by the sun,
And fairest of all shines the Drinan Donn.

The rath of the fairy, the ruin hoar,
With white silver splendour it decks them all o'er;
And down in the valleys, where merry streams run,
How sweet smells the bloom of the Drinan Donn!

Ah! well I remember the soft Spring day,
I sat by my love 'neath its sweet-scented spray;
The day that she told me her heart I had won,
Beneath the white blossoms of the Drinan Donn.

* The Brown Thorn or Sloe-tree.

The streams they were singing their gladsome song,
The soft winds were blowing the wild woods among,
The mountains shone bright in the red setting sun,
And my love in my arms 'neath the Drinan Donn.

'Tis my prayer in the morning, my dream at night,
To sit thus again by my heart's dear delight,
With her blue eyes of gladness, her hair like the sun,
And her sweet loving kisses, 'neath the Drinan Donn.

MO BHUACHAILIN BHÁN.[*]
Ralph Varian.

Mo bhuachailin bhán
Is up with the dawn,
And over the mountain, through forest and lawn :—
By green bank and slip,
Where golden flowers dip,
The dew of the morning is still on his lip.

And down by the castle, right over the hill,
Mo bhuachailin works, the brown lands to till;
But still at the dawn we meet at the slip,
Where white lilies float and golden flowers dip.

Through field as he goes,
He pulls the wild rose,
And blossoms of blue from the green rushy bawn;
But over the rose
His damask cheek glows,
And the blue eye is bright of my bhuachailin bhán.

[*] Pr. *Mo vohilleen vaun*—a "fair little boy."

He talks not like men who think woman can't know
When liberty rises or freedom is low;
And often our thoughts for old Ireland are high,
Like the sun on the mountain when painting the sky.
   My bhuachailin bhán
   Is clear as the dawn,
No shadow of falsehood to cloud his blue eye,
   The plans of Untruth
   'Tis He can confute,
And Tyranny shrinks when he stands to defy.

And sometimes his blue eyes will dream in the dawn;
And fitful and wild is mo bhuachailin bhán;—
But as Infancy kind, he is dear to my mind,
And the Shield of my life is mo bhuachailin bhán!
   Mo bhuachailin bhán

The dew on the lip of mo bhuachailin bhán
Is gossamer gold, strung with beads of the dawn;
What hard heart shall dare to brush them away?
No hard heart but mine, at the dawning of day!
   Mo bhuachailin bhán.

SPIRIT-COMPANY.
Thomas Irwin.

Up cheerful as the morn I rise,
 Though foreign airs around me blow,
For well I deem that Spirit-eyes
 Look into mine where'er I go:

So, in the viny window nook,
    With southern sunlight round, I sit,
And read aloud, from some old book,
    Old music-lines of poet-wit,
That those I love around may hear me,
And melt in sweet mute laughters near me.

With them I stroll all day along
    The fresh blue bay and sunny shore,
And hear the brown old fisher's song,
    Above his nets hummed o'er and o'er;
And wander up the evening cliffs,
    Askirted by the shadowy limes;
And as I watch the fading skiffs,
    I whisper o'er of loved old times,
That those I love around may hear me,
And smile with gentle memories near me.

And when the golden sunset dips
    Beneath the garden's walnut trees,
In vintage gay I bathe my lips,
    Till the white star floats up the seas:
Then as upon the hill o'er head,
    The quiet shepherd pens his fold,
I sit among the stilly Dead,
    And sing the songs they loved of old,
And hear their echoes, grown divine,
Come back through this waked heart of mine.

But when o'er hill and ocean soon
    Falls the deep midnight blue and rare,
And tolling bell and rounded moon
    Awake the trancèd time of prayer—

Through starry casement lone I gaze
    Upon the heavenly path they trod,
And murmur o'er their love and praise,
    With lowly knee before our God :
And hear as though beyond the sea,
The loved Old Voices pray for me.

ARTHUR M'COY.
1798.
ANONYMOUS.

While the snow-flakes of winter are falling
    On mountain, and house-top, and tree,
Come olden weird voices recalling
    The homes of Hy-Faly to me.
The ramble by river and wild wood,
    The legends of mountain and glen,
When the bright magic mirror of childhood
    Made heroes and giants of men.

Then I had my dreamings ideal,
    My prophets and heroes sublime,
Yet I found one, true, living and real,
    Surpass all the fictions of time :
Whose voice thrilled my heart to its centre,
    Whose form tranced my soul and my eye,
A temple no treason could enter ;
    My hero was Arthur M'Coy.

For Arthur M'Coy was no bragger,
    No bibber, no blustering clown,
'Fore the club of an ale-house to swagger,
    Or drag his coat-tail through the town ;

But a veteran stern and steady,
  Who felt for the land and her ills;
In the hour of her need ever ready
  To shoulder a pike for the hills.
As the strong mountain tower spreads its arms,
  Dark, shadowy, silent, and tall,
In our tithe-raids and midnight alarms,
  His bosom gave refuge to all:
If a mind clear, and calm, and expanded,
  A soul ever soaring and high,
'Mid a host—gave a right to command it—
  A hero was Arthur M'Coy.

Whilst he knelt, with a christian demeanour,
  To his priest, or his Maker, alone,
He scorned the vile slave, or retainer,
  That crouched round the castle or throne.
The Tudor, The Guelph, The Pretender,
  Were tyrants, alike, branch and stem;
But who'd free our fair land, and defend her
  A nation, were monarchs to him.

And this faith in good works he attested,
  When Tone linked the true hearts, and brave,
Every billow of danger he breasted—
  His sword-flash, the crest of its wave;
A standard he captured in Gorey;
  A sword-cut, and ball through the thigh,
Were among the mementoes of glory
  Recorded of Arthur M'Coy.

Long the guest of the law and its beagles,
  His covert the cave and the tree;
Though his home was the home of the eagles,
  His soul was the soul of the free.

No toil, no defeat could enslave it,
   Nor franchise, nor " Amnesty Bill"—
No lord, but the Maker who gave it,
   Could curb the high pride of his will.

With the gloom of defeat ever laden—
   Seldom seen at the hurling or dance,
Where, through blushes, the eye of the maiden
   Looks out for her lover's advance;
And whenever he stood to behold it,
   A curl of the lip or a sigh,
Was the silent reproach that unfolded
   The feelings of Arthur M'Coy.

For it told him of freedom o'ershaded—
   That the iron had entered their veins—
When beauty bears manhood degraded,
   And manhood's contented in chains.
Yet he loved that fair race as a martyr,
   And if his own death could recall
The blessing of liberty's charter,
   His bosom had bled for them all.

And he died for his love—I remember,
   On a mound by the Shannon's blue wave,
On a dark snowy eve in December,
   I knelt at the patriot's grave.
The aged were all heavy-hearted—
   No cheek in the church-yard was dry:
The sun of our hills had departed—
   God rest you, old Arthur M'Coy!

I'M VERY HAPPY WHERE I AM.*

A Peasant Woman's song. 1864.

Dion Boucicault.†

I'm very happy where I am,
    Far across the say,
I'm very happy far from home,
    In North Amerikay.

It's only in the night, when Pat
    Is sleeping by my side,
I lie awake, and no one knows
    The big tears that I've cried;

For a little voice, still calls me back
    To my far, far counthrie,
And nobody can hear it spake,
    Oh! nobody but me.

There is a little spot of ground
    Behind the chapel wall,
It's nothing but a tiny mound,
    Without a stone at all;

---

* "A few days ago," says Boucicault, "I stood on the North Wall and witnessed the emigrant, embarking for the Far West, as I have often stood on the quays of New York to see them arrive in America. While chewing the cud of many sweet and bitter fancies over this sad review, and picturing to myself the fate of each group as it passed, a chord in the old harp which every Irishman wears in his breast, twanged in a minor key, and I heard a young Irish wife in the backwoods of Ohio singing this strain."

† An Irish-American, Author of the popular drama "The Colleen Bawn"—from Gerald Griffin's Irish novel of "The Collegians."

It rises like my heart just now,
  It makes a dawny hill;
It's from below the voice comes out,
  I cannot kape it still.

Oh! little Voice; ye call me back
  To my far, far counthrie,
And nobody can hear ye spake,
  Oh! nobody but me.

AN CAILIN DEAS.
Anonymous.
From a New York Paper.

A fig for your pikes and your rifles;
  More dear to my passionate care
The tiniest glance of the trifles,
  That flashes from Kathaleen's hair.
Her voice like a rivulet gushing,
  Would silence the minstrel of dawn,
While cheating the kine she is hushing,
  When milking on Carigeen's lawn.

Her brow than the snow-flake is whiter,
  Her cheeks flushed with tint of the rose,
Her eye than the morning star brighter,
  And her hair black and lustrous as sloes.
She trips o'er the cowslips so lightly,
  As scarcely their down to remove,
And her billowy bosom heaves slightly,
  As if with the echoes of love.

You follow the green banner streaming,
  And climb to the summit of fame:
My star is my darling's eye beaming,
  My glory her love-lighted fame.
Place cannon and rifle before me,
  And Kathleen behind their array,
Although into ribbons they tore me,
  I'd bear my loved darling away!

THERE ARE VOICES I WEEN HYMNING HOPE IN THE SKIES.

ANONYMOUS.

From an Irish-American Paper.

AIR—"The Last Rose of Summer."

There are voices I ween hymning hope in the skies;
Where the bird of red plume through the blue azure flies;
And the harp-strings that thrilled to my touch long ago,
With the spirit of song, once again are aglow.
Strike the chords, for the warrior's spirit anew
In the battle's red glare flash again on my view;
Yes, I see the proud chiefs, death, they told me could chain,
In their vigour, and manhood, and splendour again.

Men oft' told me they died, but I knew 'twas untrue,
For their prowess, nor heaven nor earth could subdue;
And when even the soul quits the invisible form,
They still live in the sunbeams, and ride on the storm:

And the breath of the tempest, when flinging its
  gage
On the down-tumbled forest but mimics its rage,
And the white-handed maidens—but ah, 'tis a
  dream !
'Tis *the* dream where the past, its illusions still beam;

'Tis a dream, did I say ?—yet I hear once again,
Ringing clear on my ear the prophetical strain ;
And it comes in such fulness of life and of truth
As once more to revive the fond longings of youth.
'Tis a dream ? never dream of so truthful a dye,;
On the eye of the sleeper beamed down from the sky,
'Tis the light of young Liberty's first flashing ray,
Ere it bursts on the isle in the full flush of day.

MUSIC IN THE STREET.

ANONYMOUS.

Suggested by hearing " Patrick's day" and " Garry-
owen" played on the fourth of July by the band of the
60th Regiment, in the streets of New York.

It rose upon the sordid street,
  A cadence sweet and lone ;
Through all the vulgar din it pierced,
  That low melodious tone.
It thrilled on my awakened ear
  Amid the noisy mart,
Its music over every sound
  Vibrated in my heart.

I've heard full oft a grander strain
　　Through lofty arches roll,
That bore on the triumphant tide
　　The rapt and captive soul.
In this the breath of my own hills
　　Blew o'er me soft and warm,
And shook my spirit, as the leaves
　　Are shaken by the storm.

As sounds the distant ocean wave
　　Within a hollow shell,
I heard within this far off strain
　　The gentle waters swell
Around my distant island shore,
　　And glancing through the rocks,
While o'er their full and gliding wave
　　The sea-birds wheeled in flocks.

There, through the long delicious eves,
　　Of that old haunted land,
The Naiads in their floating hair
　　Yet dance upon the strand.
Till near and nearer came the sound,
　　And swelled upon the air,
And still strange echoes trembled through
　　The magic music there.

It rose above the ceaseless din,
　　It filled the dusty street,
As some cool breeze of freshness blows
　　Across the desert's heat.
It shook their squalid attic homes—
　　Pale exiles of our race—
And drew to dingy window panes
　　Full many a faded face.

And eyes whose deep and lustrous light
  Flashed strangely, lonely there,
And many a young and wistful brow
  Beneath its soft brown hair ;
And other eyes of fiercer fire,
  And faces rough and dark,
Brave souls ! that bore thro' all their lives
  The tempests on their bark.

In through the narrow rooms it poured,
  That music sweeping on,
And perfumed all their heavy air
  With flowers of summers gone,—
With waters sparkling to the lips,
  With many a summer breeze,
That woke into one rippling song
  The shaken summer trees.

In it, along the sloping hills
  The blue flax blossoms bent ;
In it, above the shining streams
  The " Fairy Fingers" leant ;
In it, upon the soft green Rath,
  There bloomed the Fairy Thorn ;
In their tired feet they felt the dew
  Of many a harvest morn.

In it, the ripe and golden corn
  Bent down its heavy head—
In it, the grass waved long and sweet
  Above their kindred dead—
In it, the voices of the loved
  They might no more behold,
Came back and spoke the tender words
  And sang the songs of old.

Sometimes there trembled through the strain
  A song like falling tears,
And then it rose and burst again
  Like sudden clashing spears;
And still the faces in the street,
  And at the window panes,
Would cloud or lighten, gloom or flash,
  With all its changing strains.

But ah! too soon it swept away,
  That pageantry of sound,
Again the parted tide of life
  Closed darkly all around.
As in the wake of some white bark,
  In sunshine speeding on,
Close in the dark and sullen wave,
  The darker where it shone.

The faces faded from my view,
  Like faces in a dream;
To its dull channel back again
  Crept the subsiding stream.
And I too starting like the rest,
  Cast all the spell aside,
And let the fading music go—
  A blossom down the tide.

OSCAR—THE DOG OF SHAUN DESMOND.
Ralph Varian.

Through meadows of gay Inniscarra,
    Where feathered grass dips at the rim,
And shadowy trout, like an arrow,
    Send bubbles to play at the brim;

The daisy-fields blinked to the morning,
    And stooped to the west every night;
The freshest of perfume adorning
    Wide bunches that yielded delight.

And joy, from the bright silver quiver,
    Of trout low, or sky-cleaving lark;
Bright shades in the sky and the river,
    Enkindle the love-heaving spark.

And Nancy, and Norah together,
    Led fairy-troops over the hill;
They wound through the moss and the heather,
    And meadow-insh down by the rill.

The fern, on the hillocks surrounding,
    Is stirring, a bright heaving sea,
And through it comes, dipping and bounding,
    Some object its course cleaving free.

'Tis Oscar, the dog of Shaun Desmond,
    With osier-wand basket of white,
Of him, the bright children are *so* fond,
    They meet him with boundless delight.

In his basket they place the white biscuit,
    And butter, and bottle of milk;
Suspended from white neck, they risk it,
    It rests on his coating of silk.

And Oscar returns to his master,
  Who lives in the cave by the rill;
No pigeon could, safer or faster,
  Bear message o'er moorland and hill.

The children sit down by a hayrick,
  To hear of the beautiful hound;
The tale of Shaun Desmond, from Patrick,
  Where woodruff wafts perfume around.

" Forget not, my children, the outlaw,
  Who saving the Poor from the Great,
Avenging their sad wrongs without law,
  Was forced to a desolate fate."

He tells how they outlawed Shaun Desmond,
  For shooting some tyrannous slave;
And forced him, for shelter, where rush-wand,
  And osiers are fringing the wave.

" This dog to Shaun Desmond was given,
  With good sense, far more than a hound;
He sure was inspired by kind Heaven
  To steer safe, where dangers abound!

" Like manna, soft falling at evening,
  The Jews in the desert to save;
Or raven, with bread, swiftly winging,
  To succour the saint in his cave."

A tear gems the clear eye of Childhood,
  As dew when the speedwell is shut,
Or gems, of the glittering wild wood,
  When Autumn drops down the brown nut.

But songs of the sunshine will come quick
  On Childhood's sweet April showers,
And Patrick just tossing the hayrick
  Found laughter ring out from its bowers.

But flinging the hay from their curls,
  The children are serious again,
And say that no treacherous churls
  Shall win Oscar's secret from them.

" My children, through life while you're steering,
  May this in your good hearts endure,
Oh, seek to secure for Dear Erinn,
  Fixed homes for her labouring poor !

" Now think of good Oscar each morning
  And bear him the napkin of food,
And give him the fair timely warning
  If Red Coats appear near the wood."

They talk of the faithful Dumb Creature,
  As homeward they leisurely pace,
And find, in the bosom of nature,
  Sweet lessons no time can efface.

SHAUN'S HEAD.

Scene :—*Before Dublin Castle*—Night—a Clansman of Shaun O'Neil's discovers his Chief's head on a pole.

JOHN SAVAGE.

God's wrath upon the Saxon ! may they never know the pride
Of dying on the battle-field, their broken spear beside ;

When victory gilds the gory shroud of every fallen brave,
Or death no tales of conquered clans can whisper to his grave.
May every light from Cross of Christ that saves the heart of man,
Be hid in clouds of blood before it reach the Saxon clan;
For sure, O God!—and you know all whose thought for all sufficed—
To expiate these Saxon sins, they'd want another Christ.

Is it thus, O Shaun the haughty! Shaun the valiant! that we meet—
Have my eyes been lit by Heaven but to guide me to defeat;
Have *I* no chief—or *you* no clan, to give us both defence,
Or must I, too, be statued here with thy cold eloquence?
Thy ghastly head grins scorn upon old Dublin's Castle-tower,
Thy shaggy hair is wind-tossed, and thy brow seems rough with power;
Thy wrathful lips, like sentinels, by foulest treachery stung,
Look rage upon the world of wrong, but chain thy fiery tongue.

That tongue whose Ulster accent woke the ghost of Columbkill,
Whose warrior words fenced round with spears the oaks of Derry Hill;

Whose reckless tones gave life and death to vassals
and to knaves,
And hunted hordes of Saxons into holy Irish
graves.
The Scotch marauders whitened when his war-cry
met their ears,
And the death-bird, like a vengeance, poised above
his stormy cheers;
Ay, Shaun, across the thundering sea, out-chanting
it your tongue,
Flung wild un-Saxon war-whoopings the Saxon
Court among.

Just think, O Shaun,! the same moon shines on
Liffey as on Foyle,
And lights the ruthless knaves on both, our kins-
men to despoil;
And you the hope, voice, battle-axe, the shield of
us and ours,
A murdered, trunkless, blinding sight above these
Dublin towers.
Thy face is paler than the moon, my heart is paler
still—
My heart? I had no heart—'twas yours—*'twas*
yours! to keep or kill.
And you kept it safe for Ireland, Chief—your life,
your soul, your pride—
But they sought it in thy bosom, Shaun—with
proud O'Neill it died.
You were turbulent and haughty, proud, and keen
as Spanish steel
But who had right of these, if not our Ulster's
Chief—O'Neill?

Who reared aloft the "Bloody Hand" until it
  paled the sun,
And shed such glory on Tyrone, as chief had never
  done.
He was "turbulent" with traitors—he was
  "haughty" with the foe—
He was "cruel," say ye Saxons! Ay! he dealt
  ye blow for blow!
He was "rough" and "wild," and who's not wild
  to see his hearthstone razed?
He was "merciless as fire"—ah, ye kindled him
  —he blazed!
He was "proud:" yes, proud of birthright, and
  because he flung away
Your Saxon stars of princedom, as the rock does
  mocking spray.
He was wild, insane for vengeance—ay! and
  preached it till Tyrone
Was ruddy, ready, wild too, with "Red hands" to
  clutch their own.

"The Scots are on the border, Shaun"—ye saints,
  he makes no breath—
I remember when that cry would wake him up
  almost from death:
Art truly dead and cold? O Chief! art thou to
  Ulster lost?
"Dost hear, *dost hear?* By Randolph led, the
  troops the Foyle have crossed!"
He's truly dead! he must be dead! nor is his
  ghost about—
And yet no tomb could hold his spirit tame to such
  a shout:

The pale face droopeth northward—ah! his soul
   must loom up there,
By old Armagh, or Antrim's glynns, Lough Foyle,
   or Bann the Fair!
I'll speed me Ulster-wards, your ghost must wander
   there, proud Shane,
In search of some O'Neill, through whom to throb
   its hate again.

LAND-LAW RHYME.
Isaac Stephen Varian.
A BALLAD OF '48.

O! peacefully the sun went down,
   And sweetly shone the stars,
And softly rose the silent moon:
   No sound the stillness mars.

The cabins on the hillock's slope
   Repose near rip'ning grain;
Green kitchen-garden, fruit-ground, field,
   And sheep-strewn cattle plain

These cabins seem a slumbering part
   Of nature, free from strife;
Without a wreath of smoke, or stir,
   Or dog, or village life.

O! wearily the sun goes down—
   O! wearily fades the light—
O! wearily the silent stars
   Gleam through the dreary night.

Nor moon, nor stars, nor human eye,
  Sees a lone watcher bide—
There—kneeling—with the putrid dead,
  The dying by her side !

Is there not one kind neighbour near
  The scalding tear to dry ?
" O ! Holy Mother—hear my prayer—
  Father above—we die !

" Speak to me—Norah—Mavourneen—
  Machree-thu ! speak to me—
O ! blessed angels, is she gone ?—
  Is no one left to me ?"

O ! wearily the night moaned on—
  O ! wearily dawned the light—
O ! wearily the watcher looked—
  Upon that wretched night !

*   *   *   *   *   *
  *   *   *   *   *

THE SUNNY SOUTH SO GLOWING.
Andrew Orr, (Australia.)

The sunny South is glowing in the glow of Southern glory,
  And the Southern Cross is waving o'er the freest of the free ;
Yet vain, in vain, my weary heart would try to hide the story
  That evermore 'tis wandering back, dear native land, to thee :

The heathy hills of Malazan, the Bann's translucent
　　waters,
　　Glenleary's shades of hazel, and Agivy's winding
　　　　streams ;
And Kathleen of the raven locks, the flower of Erinn's
　　daughters,—
　　Lost heaven of wildering beauty ! thou art mine
　　　　at least in dreams.
　　　　　　Oh ! the green land, the old land,
　　　　　　Far dearer than the gold land,
With all its landscape glory and unchanging sum-
　　mer skies ;
　　　　　　Let others seek their pleasures
　　　　　　In the chase of golden treasures,
Be mine a dream of Erinn and the light of Kathleen's
　　eyes.

Sweet scenes may group around me, hill and dale,
　　lagoon and wildwood,
　　And eyes as bright and cloudless, as the azure
　　　　skies above ;
But strange the face of nature—not the happy
　　haunts of childhood,
　　And cold the glance of beauty—not the smile of
　　　　early love ;
Even in the pulse of joy itself, the native charm is
　　wanting,
　　For distant far the bosoms that would share it
　　　　as their own ;
Too late to learn that loving hearts will never bear
　　transplanting,
　　Uprooted once, like seedless flowers, they wither
　　　　lost and lone.

Oh! the old land, the green land,
That land of lands the queen land;
Keep, keep the gorgeous splendour of your sunny
    Southern shore ;
    Unfading and undying,
    O'er the world between us lying,
The hallowed loves of former days are mine for
    evermore.

Ballarat, Dec. 1860

HE BUILT ME A LIGHT BOAT.
RALPH VARIAN.
(*To a child*)
AIR—"Oh! we went boating."

He built me a light boat—wasn't she a tight boat?
    With wings like a bird, the first of the flock;
He came, without warning, in the grey morning,
    And tapped at my window, with a soft knock:
      And we went boating—and we went sporting,
      Oh! we went boating down to Blackrock!

Graceful and sprightly— stepping politely—
    Hand on the gate—unbolting the lock—
Then, like a ring-dove, up through the spring-grove
    Where the green holly hangs from the rock:
      And we went boating. &c.

Passing Cork City—looking so pretty —
    Where the great vessels rest in the dock;
Under the highland, down by the island,
    Landing me safely on the grey rock:
      And we went boating, &c.

Pleasant the boating—gliding and floating
   Close to the castle, down by the loch;
Convent, and spire, and hills of Glanmire,
   And the sweet shady woods of Blackrock.
     And we went boating, &c.

O, it was pleasant, when a poor peasant,
   Dressed us a salmon, caught in the loch;
Where the Arbutus' blossoms are beauteous,
   Kindling a fire beneath the grey rock:
     And we went boating, &c.

And in the evening Andy was grieving,
   When we set sail at six of the clock;
Sunset was glorious—song-birds uproarious,
Crying—" leave not the woods of Blackrock!"
     And we went boating, &c.

The moon rose in splendour—breezes were tender,
   Wafting our sails away from the loch;
Soft breezes failing, and to keep sailing,
   We had to row away from Blackrock:
     And we went boating, &c.

In years upon years, in smiles or in tears,
   I'll never forget the woods of Blackrock;
Nor my own Andy, who was a dandy,
   And took me boating down to Blackrock!
     And we went boating—and we went sporting,
     Oh, we went boating down to Blackrock!

THE MARTYR.
ANONYMOUS (TYRIA.)

On the dread tempest-wing over the stormy sea,
    And fearful paths untrod
Past ships and fleets, whose pride and chivalry,
    Bowed to the might of God,
From the far, jewelled "Eldorado" of the west—
To a dethronéd queen's poor hopeless breast,
    Came news that darkly bode.

The tale to her bleeding heart is quickly told—
    Her exiled son is dead—
Deep, in the starry land of corn and gold,
    They've pillowed his weary head;
There,'neath the hickory trees and waving limes,
And hemlocks dark, where creeping ivy climbs,
    Is made his dreamless bed.

He sunk to rest, with hopeful, trusting prayer,
    For his queen Mother-land—
She, for whose weal his fiery love did dare
    Fetters and felon brand;
In his proud youth his hopes were round her wreathed,
And his last sigh of ebbing life was breathed—
    For her, proscribed and banned.

Now from her bruised heart the poor lorn queen,
    Over the wild sea's surge,
Pours out, with pallid lips, the dismal caoine—
    Her dead son's dirge;
List! O ye throned heavens, to her song of woe,
Pity her anguish'd soul—her tears that flow—
    Avert thy scourge.

*   .   .   .   .   .

" My son is dead!—my beautiful, my brave,
    Gone to hi speaceful sleep.
And strangers laid my darling in his grave :
    Therefore, I moan and weep.
Oh! how he loved me—oh! but his heart was true,
And his words were balm, soft as the blessed dew
    On the harebells deep.

" In the dim future time, when of the garish throng
    Who sought in tinselled state
Thy brave heart's blood—sought it through crime
    and wrong,
    And perjury and hate;
When, of their paltry thrones no trace survive
In song and story, TERENCE!*thy name shall live
    Godlike and pure, and great.

" Ye stately towering pines, ye golden orange trees,
    Bending his grave above,
With dreamy music in the mournful breeze,
    Sigh o'er my dear, dead love.
Oh mystic, trackless sea, sing in your ceaseless roll,
A holy requiem for the patriot's soul—
    Droop, lilies of the grove.

" Ah! my dear darling, had but thy dying eyes
    When set their sun,
Been closed by me, thy mother, 'midst my sighs,
    My own, my gallant one!
I would have hushed thee to thy final rest,
And, shamrock-shrouded, wrapt thee in my breast—
    God's will be done."

      •   •   •   •   •

    * Terence Bellew Mac Manus.

Young men of Erinn!—ye of the old proud race,
    Sons of the fiery Gael!
The hapless queen who sings, with shadowed face,
    Her sad death-wail;
Whose cry is borne across the troubled sea,
Is she who bore—who nursed ye tenderly—
    Your mother, Innisfail.

And he, whose ashes lie in the golden sand,
    Where the red sun sinks down,
Who, throned on high, shall in the spirit land
    Receive a martyr-crown—
He was thy brother. Go thou and do and dare
Like him, thy guiding star; for Ireland, sweet and
  fair,
    Win glory and renown.

CAITLIN TIRRIAL.
FROM THE IRISH. GEORGE SIGERSON, TRANSLATOR.
Air—" Cáitlin Tirrial."*

'Tis my joy to sing of all beings fair,
And 'tis time to sing Kate of the curling hair;
For of all the fair maidens that ever were seen,
I never knew one like my bonnie Caitlin! †

---

  * "Kathleen Trecal," or "Kitty Tyrrel."
  † Commonly written *Kathleen*, and pronounced like
"*Caut-leen.*" But it is nearly impossible to represent
the delicate liquid sound of the *t* and *l* by English
letters.

'Tis my ruin of heart each day-dawn gray,
That I'm not by Loch Erril's side far away,
For there I might hope to behold on the green,
The bloom of its lily-flowers—bonnie Caitlin!

I have never seen Night in its cloudiness
So dark as her clustering curling tress;
O, if I could win her and wed her—my queen,
The seas I'd sail over with bonnie Caitlin!

She's more red than the sunset, more bright than
  the swan,
And song, like her sweet voice, I never heard one!
There's not in my pulses a red drop so mean
Would not flow to defend thee, my bonnie Caitlin!

O, bonnie Caitlin—O, my bonnie Caitlin!
Could I see her once more by the holly-bush green,
I would lift her sad heart into gladness serene,
I would steal from her cruel kin bonnie Caitlin!

I've read thy dear letter upon the hill lea,
Than "the music of fairies," 'twas sweeter to me;
O, the cause of much grief—for long sad have I
  been—
And the sole joy of life is my bonnie Caitlin!

DAVIS.

WRITTEN ON SEEING THE STATUE IN MOUNT JEROME.

ANONYMOUS.

I stand beside thy tomb,
  Lost Chieftain of our race—
No dull abode of gloom,
  This thy last resting place;

The golden sunlight streams
  Upon that marble brow;
And there, in fancy's dreams,
  Bright thoughts seem gathering now.
Brother bards have sung thy nation's anguish-moan;
A kindred soul impressed thy form upon the stone!

But oh! the kindling glance,
  The lovelight of thine eye;
Thy footsteps firm advance,
  The greeting or reply—
The hand of friendly grasp,
  The voice of thrilling tone—
Within death's leaden clasp
  All these, alas! are gone!
And yet! thy lightning thoughts still our hearts shall warm,
And be to Freedom's barque a life-light in the storm.

Full fain would I believe,
  That o'er the poet's grave,
The fading hues of eve,
  Their softest shadows weave.
And when at midnight dim,
  Wild tempests groaning rise;
That, piercing wails for him,
  Ascend the darkened skies:
But sweeter 'tis to know his spirit lives enshrined
Within a Nation's heart—and in his People's mind.

THE IRISH MOTHER'S LAMENT.

ELIZABETH WILLOUGHBY TREACY.*

I'm kneeling by your grave, aroon ! the autumn
  sun shines bright,
Flinging upon the grassy mound a flood of golden
  light ;
The flowers I tended for your sake are dropping
  one by one,
While I must weep in hopeless grief above your
  grave, my son.

The withered leaves are showering down, they
  cannot break your rest ;
And fair and bright the gorgeous pall they've
  flung upon your breast :
I saw them bud and blossom forth, beneath the soft
  spring sky,
But little dreamed that you, my son, should be the
  first to die !

I knew that want had paled your cheek, that hunger
  cast its blight
Upon the crimson lip, and eye, whose very glance
  was light !
I knew the powerful arm grew weak, the sweet
  voice lost its tone ;
Yet still watched on, in trembling fear, till death the
  struggle won.

* Ballymena, Co. Antrim, author of a little volume of patriotic poems, published in Belfast.

I longed to yield with cheerfulness the treasure lent
  to me,
But vainly strove to bow the will, although I
  bent the knee!
Oh! terrible the inward strife that rends the
  mother's heart.
They only know who've felt the pang, how hard it
  is to part.

Was there not plenty in the land? the earth gave
  forth her store—
The glad and fruitful mother earth, with riches
  brimming o'er;
Not for the slave who tilled the soil the garnered
  wealth was won;
Our tyrant masters gorged their fill, and murdered
  thee, my son!

Were there not stately homes enough, that our
  rooftree must fall?
On the forsaken green hill-side I see the
  blackened wall;
Be calm, my heart, in faith abide, God will not
  still endure,
That tyrant hands shall desecrate the dwellings of
  the poor:

The dwellings of the virtuous poor, the homes of
  poverty,
Are sacred in the sight of God, though humble
  they may be;
Beneath the holy cabin roof the truest prayers
  may rise,
And many a suffering spirit there, is fashioned for
  the skies.

Mavourneen! hark, the bitter winds are howling
  round your home,
Sleep on in peace, my own one, sleep, your mother
  soon will come;
The autumn leaves are showering down upon your
  place of rest,
And bright and beautiful the pall that wraps your
  gentle breast.

THE WESTERN WINDS.
Anonymous.

A maiden sat on an ocean-steep,
  She gazed on the place where the sun went down;
Her face was mild as an infant's sleep,
  Her silken hair was a wavy brown.
    She murmured sadly, softly, and low,
      As the soothing tone of the gentle dove—
    "Of all the winds the heaven can blow,
      The west, the west, is the one I love.

"Last night I dreamed that a summer eve
  Brought back my long lost love to me;
He clasped me close and 'No longer grieve,'
  He whispered me softly, 'a stór mo chree.'
    Alas, alas!" and her voice was low
      As the plaintive tone of the gentle dove—
    "The sun is gone, and the West winds blow,
      Yet where, oh where is my plighted love?

"'Tis a long dark dream, like a funeral hymn;
  Will it ever end, will it pass away?
My heart is sad, and my eyes are dim;
  Will it ever behold hope's dawning day?"

Her voice sank down to an accent low
   As the soothing tone of the gentle dove—
"How sweet the rush of the west winds blow!
   But where ah! where is my only love?

"If Eoghan comes, will he bring to me
   The heart that away from Erin he bore?
They say that all in that land are free,
   And perhaps he may love its maidens more.
     Oh no, oh no!" she murmured low,
       As soft as the tone of the plaintive dove,
    "The western wind is the one I know
      That will bear me homeward the heart I love.

"Sad was the hour that saw him sail—
   'Twas for life, dear life, he was forced to flee—
Dark was the ship when she bent to the gale,
   For she bore my world, my all from me.
    A stór!" she murmured sad and low,
      As the soothing tone of the gentle dove,
    "Why did not I to that black ship go,
      And be near you for ever, my absent love?"

Weep not, sweet maid, for his face you will see,
   He will clasp that hand to his own once more;
He will tread o'er his native hills as free
   As he does even now on the distant shore—
      For their ranks are full, and their hearts are true,
        And their arms are young and bold and brave;
     We will see their ships when the sun sinks through
       The golden brim of the Western wave.

DRAHEREEN O MACHREE!*
A NEW VERSION OF A STREET BALLAD.
M. HOGAN.†

I grieve when I think of the sweet happy days of my youth,
When all the bright dreams of this faithless world seemed truth,
When I strayed through the greenwood, as gay as a midsummer bee,
In brotherly love with my Drahereen O Machree.

Together we watched the gay lark as he sung o'er his nest;
Together we lay in the sweet-scented meadows to rest;
Together we plucked the red fruit of the flowering haw-tree,
And loved as a sweetheart my Drahereen O Machree!

His form was straight as the hazel that grows in the glen,
His manners were courteous and social and gay among men;
His bosom was fair as the snow on the rocks of the sea;
His God's brightest image was Drahereen O Machree!

He went to the wars when proud England united with France—
His regiment was first in the red battle charge to advance,

---

* Properly: Deaṅ-ḃraṫáirín ó mo ċroiḋe, "young dear little brother of my heart."
† A tradesman of Limerick, and author of a little volume of National poems.

But when evening's pale shadows had closed o'er
    the wild bloody day,
Cold, cold on the earth lay my Drahereen O
    Machree!

O! if I were there, I'd watch o'er my darling's last
    breath—
I'd wipe his cold brow, and I'd soften his pillow of
    death,
I'd pour the hot tears of my heart-breaking anguish
    o'er thee,
Oh Blossom of Beauty, my Drahereen O Machree!

Now I'm left to weep like the sorrowful bird of
    the night;
This world and its pleasures no more shall afford
    me delight;
The dark narrow grave is the only sad refuge for
    me,
Since I lost my heart's darling, my Drahereen O
    Machree!

My soul has exhausted its treasures of tears for my
    love;
He comes to my dreams from his home in the
    regions above:
I long for the time when my soul from her prison
    is free,
To meet in those regions, my Drahereen O Machree!

THE CLARE ELECTION.*
STREET BALLAD.

FROM THE IRISH.—GEORGE SIGERSON, TRANSLATOR.

Ye bards of Kincora ! brave children of Eibir,†
If sweet be these tidings, hence famous for ever,
O, grasp your tall harps, the soft-ringing, the golden,
And waking the measures of poet-bards olden,
    The gladness and hope of green Erinn declare !
    Give praise to the dauntless uprising of Clare,
    For Vesey Fitzgerald contumely must bear ;
While crowned are O'Connell's high worth and desire, a
Member he weds with bright Silè ni Gadhra !

No chief of the hosts of brave Cairbré the royal,
Of Conn na cceud cath‡ who his foes did destroy all,
Of Crimson-branch heroes, of princely Emanians,
In Tara of great deeds—in ranks of the Fenians—
    Could equal O'Connell in pleading the right !
    Ne'er came of the warriors of Cashel a knight,
    Of those who at Achruim§ grew red in the fight,
Than He more undaunted 'mid torrents of ire, a
Beseeching the favours of Silé ni Gadhra.

* This ballad was composed in Gaehlic by Eugene O'Curry, (afterwards the eminent Professor of Irish, in the Catholic University), immediately after O'Connell's election as Member for Clare, 1828. Ireland is personified under the name of " Silé ni Gadhra," pronounced as if written " Sheela nee Guira."

† Pronounced "Eivir"—mostly written Heber by Anglo-Irish historians.

‡ Conn of the hundred battles. § Vulgò "Aughrim."

O! joyous and generous, gentle and cheering,
O! mildest and meekest, yet loreful, endearing,
That faultless, that free-hearted, frank-minded
  Maiden,
With stain, sere of sorrow, or scaith never laden,
  The blooming, the beauteous delight of us all,
  The loved of the chieftains of fair Innisfáil!
  Though pining awhile in the fetters of Gall,*
Ne'er formed the Almighty on lowland or higher, a
Fairer than thou art, my Silé ni Gadhra!

Neath sorrow in Fcilim's land Eogan's† descendants
Have long lacked their rights and their warlike
  attendants,
Have drooped in contempt, without great deeds or
  battle,
Enthralled by the vile, musty clown-herds of cattle.
  Without churches or clergy, woodland or fold,
  Without Fenians, or freedom, succour or gold,
  All houseless, all hopeless,—their friends in
    the mould;
While slavish plebeians and vassals on hire, a
Betrothal might claim from our Silé ni Gadhra!

But now, ye FREE-HEARTED! renowned for your
  bravery,
Await not from foreign aid, freedom from slavery;
But marshal your masses, and crushing feuds
  under;
The foul laws that chained you, rend, rend them
  asunder;

* Strangers, Englishmen.
† Pronounced "Owan," the chief referred to is
Eogan Mór.

O! lose not an hour, in repose or complaint,
Till bursting the Sacsanach's wrongful restraint,
Ye clear from our mother-land's fame the vile taint—
Then O! what a joy! what a sight to admire, a
Returning of FREEDOM to Silé ni Gadhra!

A TRUE STORY—CALLED MOLLY BAWN.

STREET BALLAD.

A story, a sad story, to you I will relate,
Of a beautiful young maiden, who met a woful fate;
As she walked out one evening, at the setting of the sun,
And rested in a bower, a passing shower to shun.

Young Jemmy with his gun, had been fowling all the day;
And down beside the lake he came at close of twilight grey:
Her apron being about her, he took her for a fawn,
But, alas, to his grief, twas his own Molly Bawn!

Now all ye brave young men, who go sporting with the gun,
Beware of shooting late, and grey mists about the sun—
Her apron being about her—he took her for a fawn,
But, alas, to his grief, 'twas his own Molly Bawn!

When he came to the bower, and found that it was she,
His limbs they grew feeble, his eyes they could not see;
He took her in his arms, across her uncle's lawn,
And his tears flowed like fountains on his own Molly Bawn.

Young Jemmy he went home, with his gun beneath his hand,
Sick and broken-hearted, like a felon in the land;
Crying—"Father, O, my father—by the lake—a fair white fawn—
I levelled and I shot her dead—my own Molly Bawn!"

That night to her uncle her spirit did appear,
Saying—"uncle—dearest uncle—my truelove—he is clear—
My apron being about me—he took me for a fawn—
But, alas—to his grief—'twas his own Molly Bawn!"

O, Molly was his jewel, his sweetheart and his pride!
If she had lived another year she would have been his bride:
The flower of all the valley, the pride of hut and hall—
Oh, Jemmy soon will follow his own Molly Bawn.

LOWER GLANMIRE.*

Ralph Varian.

All through the woods of Lower Glanmire
Her willing feet did never tire,
Ere he was 'whelmed, her heart's desire,
   O, gaily heaved the ocean!

But weary now the woods at noon;
O, weary droops the waning moon;
And mourns, too, the falling dew
   For gentle Dan O'Daly!

He loved the river of the hills,
He loved the million dancing rills,
The sea shore, and each flower that fills
   With sweets thy fields—Dunkathel!†

The steady strong grasp of his hand
Told how he loved the Dear Old Land,
When kindred spoke of tidings grand
   And hope for stricken Ireland!

And tender ties were round him bound,
The ties of woman's love profound,
And love, confessed, made hallowed ground
   Within thy woods—Dunkathel.*

---

* A beautiful locality near the city of Cork—close to Riverstown, with which it communicates by pleasant pathways and clear rapid streams.
† Dunkathel, close to Glanmire.

He traded to the village mill;
He bore ripe corn from the hill;
The hanging woods the balm distil
   That fanned his shining hooker!

He sailed beyond the harbour-light;
The autumn waves were capped with white;
And O, he sank, the hills in sight
   That sheltered all the village!

O, bitter wail! O, piercing cry!
No eye in all the village dry!
And long her brain and heart remain
   As cold as frozen ocean!

The Virgin with her lovely Child
Appeared above the torrents wild,
And poured the heavenly balsam mild
   Upon her stricken reason.

She moves about with noiseless feet,
And feels the consolation sweet
That, in the Tranquil Realms, she'll meet
   With him she loved so dearly.

Through hanging woods of Lower Glanmire
Her trembling feet now lag and tire;
For he is 'whelmed, her heart's desire,
   And sadly heaves the ocean!

She seeks at weary close of day
The poor old mother, blind and grey,
And talks of bright days far away,
   And him they love so dearly.

Yet weary still the woods at noon,
E'en weary droops the waning moon,
And mourns, too, the morning dew
   For gentle Dan O'Daly!

THE OUTLAW'S BRIDAL.
J. T. CAMPION.

As the torrent bounds down from the mountain
Of cloud-helmed stormy Kaigeen,
And tosses, all tawny and foaming,
Through the still glen of lone Carrageen:
So dashed a bold rider of Wicklow,
With forty stout men in his train,
From the heart of the hills, where the Spirit
Of Freedom has dared to remain!

Of grey frieze their caps and their surcoats:
Their carbines were close to their knee,
And their belts were well furnished with pistols,
Like men who knew how to be free!

Oh! grass-green the sash on their shoulders,
Their caps crested green with cockades;
And their Leader, he wore a large dagger—
The brightest and keenest of blades.

To the right ran Imael's lovely valley,
And before them was meadow and mound,
And the gallop of freemen was music
The echoes sprang out to resound!

Thou leader of horsemen! why hasten
So fleetly to Brusselstown hill?
What foemen—what yeomen await thee,
To question, in Wicklow, thy will?

No foemen or yeomen they're seeking,
Tho' furiously onward they ride?
But their Leader, he loves a young maiden,
And he's speeding to make her his bride!

" Halt !" bridles were drawn and they halted :
There's a farmstead looming ahead,
And the door of the dwelling is open ;
Now—the Leader rode forward and said :

" There's somebody seeking thee, Mary ;
" A boy who came down from Kaigeen,
" With forty brave bridesmen from Laragh,
" With cockades and crosses of green !"

Oh ! Mary came out in her beauty,
The loveliest maid of Imael ;
The loveliest flower that blossomed
In all the wild haunts of the vale.

Arrayed in an emerald habit—
And the green and the white in her hair,
The Leader, he sprang from his courser,
As light as a hawk from the air—
He pressed her fair hand to his bosom ;
She felt the big throb of his heart—
" My Mary ! I'll love thee for ever,
" Till God, on this earth, will us part !"

They led out a horse on the heather!
She patted his neck with her hand,
Then sprang on his back, like a feather,
And stood in the midst of the band!

The Leader was soon in his saddle:
"Castle Ruddery's ruins," he cried;
"The Priest's house is near to Green's river,
"And here is the ring for for my bride!"

Away dashed the cavalcade fleetly,
By beauty and chivalry led,
With their carbines aflash in the sunlight,
And the saucy cockades in their head!

The Priest he demurred and he pleaded—
The maiden she blushed and she frowned,
And the Leader of Forty felt nervous,
And tapped with his gun on the ground.
And thus went the parley, till even
Began to fall down on the glen,
And the Priest thought a matron were better
To be 'mid such wild bearded men.

They were wedded: "To horse," cried the Leader,
And the bridal pair led the hot flight;
And away rode DWYER, the Outlaw,
To his mountain-cave, back in the night!

NANO NAGLE.*

[Foundress of the Presentation and Ursuline Order of Nuns in Ireland, which are devoted chiefly to the education of the poor.]

GERALD GRIFFIN.

* * * * * *

Is no waking reserved for our sleep of despair ?
Ha, see!—there's a shooting of light in the gloom,
And the spirit of Nagle replies from the tomb.

Hail, star of the lowly ! apostle of light,
In the glow of whose fervour the cottage grew bright !
Sweet violet of Sanctity, lurking concealed,
Till the wind wafts the leaf, and the bloom is revealed ;
By the light of that glory which burst on thy youth,
In its day-dreams of pleasure, and woke it to truth,
By the tears thou hast shed, by the toil thou hast borne,
Oh, say shall our night know a breaking of morn ?

THE TAGUS, AND THE LEE.

RALPH VARIAN.

There came from Spain's old famous land,
　Where Tagus wanders free,
A lover, with a stately hand,
　And bore me from the Lee:

* There is a memoir of Nano Nagle by Dean Murphy published in Cork.

His sweet smile tempers sun with dew
   Like morning on the Lee;—
But here—though Tagus sweeps in view—
   My native hills for me!

We have a home, verandah-bright,
   With myrtles blooming fair;
A window that looks out at night
   On this clear Spanish air;
But, ah! through starting tears I see
   An em'rald green hill side,
Where I would trace the winding Lee,
   And be my Spaniard's bride!

We climb these mountain heights sublime,
   Or wander on the strand,
And gazing through the golden clime,
   We bless this glorious land!
But still the thought my bosom swells—
   O with my love to be,
And hear my native Shandon bells,
   And see the winding Lee.

By vines and groves in fruitful pride,
   Hoar cork-trees waving green,
Hang on this swelling mountain side,
   And fair paths wind between!
And streams, the fern and willow reach,
   Which never cease to flow,
Where quince, and apricot, and peach,
   And luscious melons grow!

But million berries glitter black,
  In glens, and on the height,
Where ash trees shade the sunset track,
  And furze are golden bright!
And currants glitter white and red,
  In sweet flowers hums the bee,
Where strawberries, in hanging beds,
  Look down upon the Lee!

There green leaves globe the noon-tide dew,
  And green crops ridge the steep,
And witching flowers of radiant hue,
  In crystal waters peep!
O, bright the morning mushroom-time,
  The speckled fields to see,
Where song-birds usher in the prime,
  Upon the banks of Lee!

The wholesome root luxuriant grows,
  And blossoms, golden-eyed,
Where gleams the cottage-board, and shews
  Such hospitable pride!
The cream and butter fresh as dew,
  All these I miss, and more,
The golden locks, and eyes of blue
  Beside the thatched-roof door!

For ah! on Graunabraugher-height
  A child I used to be!
That beauty fed my infant-sight—
  The lough—the distant sea—
The streets of Cork—the quays—the spires,
  All rising fair to see,
The wooded hills of Lower Glanmire,
  Above the winding Lee!

The sun in splendid colours bright,
    Dips in this Tagus-bay;
The moon and stars look out at night,
    And play as bright as day;
And our verandah-window shows
    These glories fair—and more—
The orange flowers and sweet musk-rose
    Around our trellised door.

Yet dearer far that misty light
    That steals all through the west;
With Carrigraughan's vale in sight,
    And meadows cowslip-dressed!
Once more, in arch of rainbow-light
    My native bay for me;
Or Moon, or Stars, or Clouds, or Night,
    Where flows the winding Lee!

Oft, oft our prayers together rise
    For blessings on Her head
Whose brow ascends the dewy skies
    Where emerald glories spread;
With yearnings for the dear delights
    To crown sweet liberty,
When peasant's homes are safe and bright
    Where flows the winding Lee!

My Spaniard has a fairy boat,
    With latteen sails all white;
In which, with me, he loves to float
    Upon the Tagus bright;
But I would rather sail the wave,
    Or with him wander free,
On lands which hold my father's grave
    Where flows the winding Lee!

THE IRISH RAPPAREES.
A PEASANT BALLAD OF 1691.
CHARLES GAVAN DUFFY.

[When Limerick was surrendered, and the bulk of the Irish army took service with Louis XIV., a multitude of the old soldiers of the Boyne, Aughrim, and Limerick, preferred remaining in the country at the risk of fighting for their daily bread; and with them some gentlemen, loath to part from their estates or their sweethearts, among whom Redmond O'Hanlon is perhaps the most memorable. The English army and the English law drove them by degrees to the hills, where they were long a terror to the new and old settlers from England, and a secret pride and comfort to the trampled peasantry who loved them even for their excesses. It was all they had left to take pride in.]

Righ Shemus* he has gone to France, and left his crown behind :—
Ill luck be theirs, both day and night, put runnin' in his mind !
Lord Lucan† followed after, with his Slashers brave and true,
And now the doleful keen is raised—" What will poor Ireland do ?
      What must poor Ireland do ?
Our luck," they say," has gone to France—what *can* poor Ireland do ?"

---

* " Righ Seamus"—King James II.
† After the Treaty of Limerick, Patrick Sarsfield, Lord Lucan, sailed with the brigade to France, and was killed whilst leading his countrymen to victory at the battle of Landen, in the Low countries, on 29th July, 1693; saying, as he drew his hand, covered with his heart's blood, from his bosom, and looking at it—"Would that this were for my native land !"

Oh never fear for Ireland, for she has so'gers still,
For Rory's boys are in the wood, and Remy's on the hill;
And never had poor Ireland more loyal hearts than these—
May God be kind and good to them, the faithful Rapparees!
     The fearless Rapparees!
The jewel were you, Rory, with your Irish Rapparees!

Oh, black's your heart, Clan Oliver, and cowlder than the clay!
Oh, high's your head, Clan Sassenach, since Sarsfield's gone away!
It's little love you bear to us, for sake of long ago,
But howld your hand, for Ireland still can strike a deadly blow—
     Can strike a mortal blow—
Och! *dar-a-Criost!* 'tis she that still could strike a deadly blow!

The Master's bawn, the Master's seat, a surly *bodagh* ‡ fills;
The master's son, an outlawed man, is riding on the hills.
But, God be praised, that round him throng, as thick as summer bees,
The swords that guarded Limerick wall—his loyal Rapparees!
     His lovin' Rapparees!
Who dare say *no* to Rory Oge, with all his Rapparees?

‡ "Bodagh"—A severe and inhospitable man.

Black Billy Grimes of Latnamard, he racked us long
  and sore—
God rest the faithful hearts he broke!—we'll never
  see them more!
But I'll go bail he'll break no more, while Truagh
  has gallows trees,
For why?—he met, one lonesome night, the fearless
  Rapparees!
                  The angry Rapparees!
They never sin no more, my boys, who cross
  the Rapparees!

Now, Sassenach and Cromweller, take heed of
  what I say—
Keep down your black and angry looks, that scorn
  us night and day;
For there's a just and wrathful Judge, that every
  action sees,
And He'll make strong, to right our wrong, the
  faithful Rapparees!
                  The fearless Rapparees!
The men that rode at Sarsfield's side, the roving
  Rapparees!

MICHAEL DWYER.*
T. D. SULLIVAN.

At length brave Michael Dwyer, and his undaunted
  men,
Were scented o'er the mountains, and tracked into
  the glen;

* The same 'Ninety-eight Wicklow Leader, whose life has been recently written by Dr. Campion; and whose daring has been celebrated by him, in some of his forcible Ballads, one of which we have given—" The Outlaw's Bridal."—

The stealthy soldiers followed, with ready blade
  and ball,
And swore to trap the outlaw that night in wild
  Emall.*

They prowled about the valley, and toward the
  dawn of day,
Discovered where the faithful and fearless heroes
  lay;
Around the little cottage they formed in a ring,
And called out " Michael Dwyer! Surrender to the
  king !"

Thus answered Michael Dwyer—" Into this house
  we came
Unasked by those who own it; they cannot be to
  blame;
Then let those guiltless people, unquestioned pass
  you through,
And when they're passed in safety, I'll tell you
  what we'll do."

'Twas done.—"And now," said Dwyer, " your work
  you may begin;
You are a hundred outside, we're only four within;
We've heard your haughty summons, and this is
  our reply—
We're true United Irishmen, we'll fight until we
  die."

Then burst the war's red lightning, then poured the
  leaden rain;
The hills around re-echoed, the thunder peals again;

* The Glen of Emall in the county of Wicklow.

The soldiers falling round him, brave Dwyer sees
    with pride ;
But ah! one gallant comrade is wounded by his
    side.

Yet there are three remaining, good battle still to
    do ;
Their hands are strong and steady, their aim is
    quick and true—
But hark that furious shouting the savage soldiers
    raise !
The house is fired around them !—the roof is in a
    blaze !

And brighter every moment the lurid flame arose,
And louder swelled the laughter and cheering of
        their foes ;
Then spake the brave M'Alister, the weak and
    wounded man,
"You can escape, my comrades, and this shall be
    your plan :—

"Place in my hands a musket, then lie upon the floor,
I'll stand before the soldiers and open wide the
    door ;
They'll pour into my bosom the fire of their array,
Then while their guns are empty, dash through
    them and away !"

He stood before the foemen, revealed amidst the
    flames ;
From out their levelled pieces the wished-for volley
    came;
Up sprang the three survivors, for whom the hero
    died,
But only Michael Dwyer burst through the ranks
    outside.

He baffled his pursuers, who followed like the wind,
And swam the river Slaney, and left them far
  behind ;
But many a scarlet soldier he promised soon should
  fall,
For those his gallant comrades who died in wild
  Emall.

FAREWELL TO PLEASANT ERINN.
From the Irish of Geardoit Nuinsionn (Garret Nugent.)
GEORGE SIGERSON.

[This "Farewell," so full of pathos, tenderly and nobly expressed, is even more touching from the fact of its having been composed by the author in the barque which was bearing him to exile, and when the plains and mountains of his own beloved isle were departing from his sight. The bard was one of those who became " more Irish than the Irish themselves," and was forced to flee in the gloomy days of Elizabeth —in the days of MULLACHMAST.

'Tis tearful to pass from the Hills of Fail—
  'Tis grief to leave Erinn's meads—
The odorous peaks of the gay, gold bees!
  The Isle of the bounding steeds!

But though far my course o'er the easterly sea,
  And turned from Fiontan's strand,
My heart, on this journey, it leaveth me—
  Nought is dear but my Erinn's Land!

O, Land of the rich fruit-bended trees !
  O, Land of the green, green plains !
Old dewy and fragrant country of IR,
  Of the branches and golden grains !

O, Isle of the Knightly, Isle of Saints!
   O, Banba of beautiful maids!
O, Land of the blue—the clear-leaping streams,
   Of the gold-deeded champions' blades!

If blessed by GOD be my heart's dear hope,
   I'll see thee once more, FATHER-LAND!
But I never could wish from The Stranger to come
   To where Sacsanachs base command.

It is not for the perils of far, wild seas,
   But for quitting Dun-leary I grieve!
Ah, my spirit were joyless and lifeless abroad,
   Fair Delvin* it cannot leave!

Farewell to the friends who gaze after my barque,
   Brave youths of Dun Darveis† to you!
O, Meath who art noblest! O, country of song!
   Once, Land of the Free—Adieu.

   * Delvin—County Westmeath.
   † Darveis—Meath.
   Ireland is signified by the different appellations of —"Fiontan"—"Banba"—"Ir."

GLENFLESK.*
Ralph Varian.

In grandeur Cintra's peaks arise,
  The Lisbon hills are fair;
And fruits and flowers of gorgeous dyes,
  Are heavy on the air:
And all that's rugged, wild, and, grand;
  Luxuriant, graceful, bright;
In wildering mazes, hand-in-hand,
  Unite to charm the sight
    In Cintra grand.

And yet, the little home I knew
  Beside the turbid wave;
The little home that held in view
  The outlaw's wondrous cave
For me; with plot of meadow grass,
  The old oak wood in view,
The wild and storied rugged pass,
  And flowers in sun and dew,
    In sweet Glenflesk!

The Annemore stretched north and south
  Across the saffron west;
And summer came, without a drought,
  In gold and purple dressed:
The Cruachan showed the Phil-a-dhaoun;†
  The Looah and the Clyde,

---

* Near Killarney. The river Flesk flows into the Lakes.

† The Demon's Cliff, a mass of rock which forms the face of the Cruachan mountain at the opening of the valley of the Flesk. In this mass there is a fissure known as "the Outlaw's Bed."

All splashed with foam, came coursing down,
   To join the deeper tide,
     In sweet Glenflesk!

My grandame's little cot retired
   Behind the skirting wood,
And all good things my heart desired,
   Within its four walls stood;
The bright fields, sloping southward, reached
   Flesk's soft and silvery rim,
While, with the stream, a rope-walk stretched
   In elm-shadows dim
     In sweet Glenflesk!

And up the rock my mother's cot
   Crouched in the heather bright;
The children Heaven gave her lot
   Grew in her careful sight.
But grandame's partial love was dealt
   To me, the youngest child;
O, swiftly flew the months we felt,
   All radiant-winged, and wild
     In sweet Glenflesk

Beside the low and bright turf fire,
   We listened to the store,
The magic tales that could not tire;
   We heard, and asked for more;
And " Mammy Betty" (grandame's name;
   She loved its sound from me)
Would pour wild legends, bright with fame
   On hill, and cave, and tree,
     In sweet Glenflesk!

But O, the day ! the heavy day!
  The day of bitter woes !
The roofs that sheltered our kind play ;
  Our parent's soft repose ;
Our homely prayer, our fireside peace ;
  Our hospitable board,
Were levelled low, and scarce a trace
  Of homes once snugly stored,
    In sweet Glenflesk !

Then worn with want, and wild with grief,
  My misery to enhance,
I joined beneath this Wellesley chief
  To check imperial France ;
Black fate ruled high the slaughtering hour
  I joined this Saxon band,
To pine beneath its withering power,
  Far from my native land,
    And sweet Glenflesk !

O, that with heart had sped my hand,
  With Captain Rock to roam ;
To fight through passes of our land,
  For freedom, hearth, and home :
But, here encamped with alien chiefs,
  Beneath a scorching sky,
I utter forth my useless griefs,
  As far from home I lie
    And sweet Glenflesk !

Strange glories Nature's hand can stamp,
  In mellow hues and dyes ;
At night the lucid glow-worm's lamp,
  And flickering bright fire-flies ;

The Kintas of Coolares stretch,
　With gorgeous waxen flowers,
And, bright with luscious fruit-trees, reach
　The seaward caves and towers
　　Of Cintra grand!

And yet I hope to lay my head
　Beside the outlaw's cave;
Again to see, ere life be fled,
　My native glen and wave.
O, all young men of Erinn, know
　How hard must be his fate,
Who will to foreign service go,
　Far from his native state,
　　And sweet Glenflesk!

SITTING BY THE HEARTH.
To a Little Girl.
RALPH VARIAN.
AIR—"*Over the hills and Far Away.*"

Sweet Molly *now* is on my knee —
And we will ride a race, to see
Where primroses, and daisies play—
Over the hills, and far away.
　Over the hills, and over the way,
　Over the hills, at break of day,
　We will ride, till twilight grey—
　Over the hills and far away.

The pretty cuckoo flies, and sings!
The Black-cock sails, on lazy wings;
The swallow skims, ere close of day—
Over the hills and far away.

And, with the birds, in air we'll fly,
In fairy boat, we'll sail the sky,
And, with the clouds, we'll float and play—
Over the hills and far away.

We'll call to see the bright new moon,
'Tis singing now a sweet old tune;
The only words it seems to say—
" Over the hills and far away."

My Molly plays at hide-and-seek,
Like timid hare, so soft and sleek;
Or violets that peep at " day"—
Over the hills and far away.

Molly calls for Zaac to play,
She hides her head and shouts out—day!
As cuckoo startles watchful May—
Over the hills and far away.

Molly has two soft bright eyes,
That look, as in my lap she lies,
Like stars, that wink, at dawning day—
Over the hills and far away.

My Molly has two sweet, fresh cheeks,
That brim with dew, when trouble breaks;
Like buds, in lap of balmy May—
Over the hills and far away.

My Molly has sweet hands, and feet,
With dimples, where the rose-buds meet;
She moves her lips, and seems to say—
Over the hills and far away.

* * * *

Ye Children, know, who dwell afar,
These airs we learned of Saint Finn Barr;*
He'll waft them down, at break of day—
Over the hills and far away.
  Over the hills, and over the way,
  Over the hills, at break of day;
  He'll waft them, too, at Twilight grey,
  Over the hills and far away.

THE ROBIN.
Thomas Irwin.

Amid the ivy on the tomb
  The Robin sings his winter-song,
    Full of cheerful pity;
Deep grows the evening gloom,
  Dim spreads the snows along!
    And sounds the slowly tolling bell from the
      silent city.
  Sing, sweet Robin, sing
    To One that lies below;
    Few hearts are warm above the snow
  As that beneath thy wing;
  So sing, sweet, sing
  All about the coming Spring.

When summer, with hay-scented breath,
  Shall come the mountains over,
    Sing, Robin, through the valley,
Above the tufts of flowering heath,
  And o'er the honied clover,
    Where many a bronzed and humming bee
      shall voyage musically;

---

* The patron Saint of Cork.

Sing, brown spirit, sing
Each summer evening
   When I am far away;
  I know not one I'd wish so near
  The dust I love as thou, sweet dear;
So sing, sweet, sing
Still, still about the coming Spring.

SONG OF THE GALLOPING O'HOGAN.*

Robert Dwyer Joyce.

Air.—"He thought of the Charmer, &c."

Hurra! boys, hurra! for the sword by my side,
The spur and the gallop o'er bogs deep and wide;
Hurra! for the helmet an' shining steel jack,
The sight of the spoil, an' good men at my back!
  An' we'll sack and burn for King and sireland,
  An' chase the black foe from ould Ireland!

At the wave of my sword starts a thousand good men,
And we ride like the blast over moorland an' glen—
Like dead leaves of winter, in ruin an' wrath,
We sweep the cowed Saxon away from our path.
  An' we'll sack and burn for King and sireland,
  An' chase the black foe from ould Ireland!

The herds of the foe graze at noon by the rills;
We have them at night in our camp 'mid the hills—

---

* One of the Rapparee chiefs in the time of King James the Second.

Their towns lie in peace at the eve of the night,
But they're sacked an' in flames ere the next
  mornin' light!
 An' we'll sack and burn for King and sireland,
 And chase the black foe from ould Ireland!

And so we go ridin' by night and by day,
An' fight for our country an' all the rich prey;
The roar of the battle sweet music we feel,
An' the light of our hearts is the flashin' of steel!
 An' we'll sack and burn for King and sireland,
 An' chase the black foe from ould Ireland!

SONG.

Aubrey De Vere.

[In the following beautiful Song Mr. De Vere implies an apology for the cheerful character of his fellow countrymen under suffering and slavery.]

Not always the winter! not always the wail!
 The heart heals perforce where the spirit is pure!
The apple-tree blooms in the glens of Imayle;
 The black-bird sings loud by the Slane and the
  Suir!
There are princes no more in Kincora and Tara,
But the gold-flower laughs out from the Maigue
  at Athdara;
And the Spring-tide that wakens the leaf in the
  bud,
 (Sad mother, forgive us) shoots joy through our
  blood!

Not always the winter! not always the moan!
   Our fathers they tell us in old time were free;—
Free to-day is the stag in the woods of Idrone,
   And the eagle that fleets from Loch Lein o'er
     the Lee!
The blue-bells rush up where the young May hath
   trod;
The souls of our martyrs are reigning with God!
Sad mother, forgive us! yon sky-lark no choice
Permits us.—From heaven he is crying, "Rejoice!"

THE LITTLE BLACK ROSE.*
AUBREY DE VERE.

The Little Black Rose shall be red at last;
   What made it black but the March wind dry,
And the tear of the widow that fell on it fast?—
   It shall redden the hills when June is nigh!

The Silk of the Kine shall rest at last;—
   What drove her forth but the dragon fly?
In the golden vale she shall feed full fast
   With her mild gold horn, and her slow, dark eye.

The wounded wood-dove lies dead at last!
   The pine long-bleeding, it shall not die!—
This song is secret. Mine ear it passed
   In a wind o'er the plains at Athenry.

* One of the mystical names of Ireland, as is also "The Silk of the Kine." In these beautiful lines Mr. De Vere typifies the final resurgence of Ireland. The weak creatures are easily killed—the strong—such as the pine—though it bleeds, flourishes on. The Irish lost a great battle at Athenry: "they fought with unflinching bravery," says Haverty, "but the chivalry of Connaught was crushed, and irreparable injury inflicted on the Irish cause."

THE PASS OF PLUMES.

1599

R. D. WILLIAMS.*

[Essex, in the reign of Queen Elizabeth, invaded Ireland with an army of 20,000 foot, and 2,000 horse, He marched through Munster, and the sole result of his enterprise was the reduction of two Castles, and the feigned submission of three native Chiefs. When passing through Leinster, he was harassed by the O'Moores, who made an attack upon his rear-guard, in which many of his men, and several of his officers, were killed; and among the traditional records of his visit, it is told that, from the quantity of plumes of feathers of which his soldiers were despoiled, the place of action long continued to be called "The Pass of Plumes."]

"Look out," said O'Moore, to his clansmen, "afar—
Is yon white cloud the herald of tempest or war?
Hark! know you the roll of the foreigners' drums?
By heaven! Lord Essex in Panoply comes,
With corslet, and helmet, and gay bannerol,
And the shields of the nobles with blazon and scroll;
And, as snow on the larch in December appears,
What a winter of Plumes on the forest of Spears!

---

* Educated at Carlow College. His poems indicate the possession of humour, pathos, and power; we may cite "The Taxman"—"Adieu, the Snowy Sail," and the above poem, as types of his genius. He emigrated, on the partial check of the National Movement in '48, to the United States, where he became Professor of *Belles Lettres* in the Catholic College of Mobile. He died in the year 1862, in America, in about the fortieth year of his age, leaving a wife and two children.

To the clangour of trumpets and waving of flags,
The clattering of cavalry prance o'er the crags ;
And their Plumes—By St. Kyran! false Saxon,
   ere night,
You shall wish these fine feathers were wings for
   your flight.

Shall we leave all the blood and the gold of the Pale
To be shed by Armagh and be won by O'Neil ?
Shall we yield to O'Ruark, to M'Guire, and O'Donnell,
Brave chieftains of Breffny, Fermanah, Tyrconnell ;
Yon helmets, that 'Erick'* thrice over would pay
For the Sassenach heads they'll protect not to-day ?
No ! By red Mullaghmast, fiery clansmen of Leix,
Avenge your sires' blood on their murderous race.
Now, sept of O'Moore, fearless sons of the heather,†
Fling your scabbards away, and strike home and
   together !

Then loudly the clang of commingling blows,
   Up swelled from the surrounding fields,
And the joy of a hundred trumps arose,
   And the clash of a thousand shields ;
And the long plumes danced, and the falchions rung,
   And flashed the whirled spear,
And the furious barb through the wild war sprung,
   And trembled the earth with fear ;
The fatal bolts exulting fled,
   And hissed as they leaped away ;
And the tortured steed on the red grass bled,
   Or died with a piercing neigh.

   * Fine for manslaughter in the Irish code.
   † The O'Moores wore a sprig of heather in their
helmets.

I see their weapons crimsoned—I hear the mingled
  cries
Of rage and pain and triumph, as they thunder to
  the skies.
The cooluned Kerne rushes upon armour, knight and
  mace,
And bone and brass are broken in his terrible
  embrace !

The coursers roll and struggle ; and the riders, girt
  in steel,
From their saddles, crushed and cloven, to the
  purple heather reel,
And shattered there, and trampled by the charger's
  iron hoof.
The seething brain is bursting through the crushing
  helmet's roof.
Joy ! Heaven strikes for freedom ! and Elizabeth's
  array,
With her paramour to lead 'em, are sore beset
  to-day.

Their heraldry and plumery, their coronets and mail,
Are trampled on the battle-field, or scattered on
  the gale !
As the cavalry of ocean, the living billows bound,
When lightnings leap above them, and thunders
  clang around,
And tempest-crested dazzlingly, caparison'd in spray,
They crush the black and broken rocks, with all
  their roots away ;
So charged the stormy chivalry of Erin in her ire—
Their shock the roll of ocean, their swords electric
  fire—

They rose like banded billows that, when wintry
 tempests blow,
The trembling shore, with stunning roar and dreadful wreck o'erflow.

But where they burst tremendously upon the
 bloody groun',
Both horse and man, from rere to van, like shivering barques went down.
Leave your costly Milan hauberks, haughty nobles
 of the Pale,
And your snowy ostrich feathers as a tribute to
 the Gael.
Fling away gilt spur and trinket, in your hurry,
 knight and squire,
They will make our virgins ornaments, or decor-
 ate the lyre.
Ho! Essex, how your vestal Queen will storm when
 she hears
The "mere Irish" chased her minion and his twenty
 thousand spears.

Go! tell the royal virgin that O'Moore, M'Hugh
 O'Neill,
Will smite the faithless stranger while there's steel
 in Innisfail.
The blood you shed shall only serve more deep
 revenge to nurse,
And our hatred be as lasting as the tyranny we
 curse :
From age to age consuming, it shall blaze, a quench-
 less fire,
And the son shall thirst and burn still more fiercely
 than his sire.

By our sorrows, songs, and battles—by our crom-
 leachs, raths, and towers—
By sword and chain, by all our slain—between
 your race and ours
Be naked glaives and yawning graves, and ceaseless tears and gore,
Till battle's flood wash out in blood your footsteps
 from the shore!"

NANNY'S SAILOR LAD.*
WILLIAM ALLINGHAM.

Now fare you well! my bonny ship,
   For I am for the shore :
The wave may flow, the breeze may blow,
   They'll carry me no more.

And all as I came walking
   And singing up the sand,
I met a pretty maiden,
   I took her by the hand:

But still she would not raise her head,
   A word she would not speak,
And tears were on her eyelids,
   Dripping down her cheek.

Now grieve you for your father ?
   Or husband might it be ?
Or is it for a sweetheart
   That's roving on the sea ?

---

* This has turned up in our collection of Cork and Dublin Ha'penny Ballads. It is included in Mr. Allingham's "Music Master, and other poems."

It is not for my father,
   I have no husband dear,
But oh! I had a sailor lad,
   And he is lost, I fear.

Three long years
   I am grieving for his sake,
And when the stormy wind blows loud,
   I lie all night awake.

I caught her in my arms,
   And she lifted up her eyes,
I kissed her ten times over
   In the midst of her surprise.

Cheer up, cheer up, my Nanny,
   And speak again to me;
O dry your tears, my darling,
   For I'll go no more to sea.

I have a love, a true love,
   And I have golden store;
The wave may flow, the breeze may blow,
   They'll carry me no more!

A WAIL.—1847.
Doctor Wm. Drennan.*

Lament for the land where the sunbeams wander,
   Amid shadows deeper than elsewhere fall,
And the listless winds seem to wail and ponder
   Over glories past which they can't recal.

† Son of that Dr. Drennan of 1798—who wrote the celebrated poem on the death of William Orr, and the song, "When Erin first rose," etc.

Fair are its cities, but Despair frequents them;
  From its fertile valleys must the famished flee;
And coasts safe-smiling, where the wave indents them,
    Invite, Isle of Ruin! no hope to Thee!
    Och-ōn for thee, Erinn! och-ōn a chreo!

Round thy mystic towers and cromlechs lonely
  Flit shadows majestic of chiefs and sage,
But the light on each clairseah and torque is only
  Dimly reflected to this darkened age.
Felled are thy tall trees that erst branched so boldly,
  Hushed thy sweet singers that once warbled free;
O! the bleak fortune that now clasps thee coldly!
    When, Isle of Ruin! shall it pass from thee?
    Och-ōn for thee, Erin! och-ōn a chreo!

DIRGE OF OLIFEIR GRAS.*
From the Irish of Seaan Mac Walter Walsh.
GEORGE SIGERSON, TRANSLATOR.

Dark's the cloud our mountains o'er,
A cloud that never came before;
Stern the noon-hush—broken lowly
By the Voice of Sorrow solely.

Floats the death-knell on the wind,
Grief, alas! comes close behind;
Harshly hoarse the raven's croaking
Warning that man's life is broken.

For thee, O noble youth! for thee,
Wails the *bean-sig'e* † mournfullie,

  * Oliver Grace.   † Pronounced, *ban-shee.*

In the mid-night, still and lone,
Sadly swells her caoiné's* moan.

The Rock's Son† answers to her wail,
Grieving from grey wall and vale;
The cock no longer hails the pearly
Morn, nor cheers us late or early.

Ah, my Oliféir óg! mo c'roid'e,‡
'Tis thy death wakes the wild bean-sig'e;
'Tis it that brings both night and morrow,
'Tis it that brings the bitter sorrow!

What fills thy place to us, our chief?
Nought but tears, and sobs of grief;
There's nought for us since *he* is taken,
But weeping tears, and sore heart-breaking!

Death!—thou'st smote for ever, now,
The fairest flower from highest bough;
Mo nuar! could nothing stay thy doom's tone
And save our dear one from the tombstone?

Sword of Brightness! strong and sure
Shielder of the just and poor,
'Neath thy noble father's banner
High thou won'st in Ormond, honour!

Ne'er till now—ah, ne'er till now,
Thy home 'neath hopeless grief did bow;
Good thou wast, O Heir! and noble,
Thee, they mourn in bitter trouble.

* Pron. *keena* and not *keen*, as it is generally mis-spelt.
† Son of the rock is the literal meaning of *Mac Alla*, the Irish for *echo*.
‡ Pronounced *mochree*, i.e. young Oliver, my heart!

Rightful heir, in truth—still bearing
High their name and love for Erinn;
As oak-tree, thou wast fair to see,
And like to broaden thy branches free.

Such was not thy fate's designing,
Lorn in earth thou'rt now reclining;
O, Ruin of Joy, each day for all—
Ah—for thy love —a black heart-pall!

She, a mother, ever weepeth
For the long, long sleep, he sleepeth,
Her children's sire, her first love, dearest—
Ah, 'tis she hath anguish drearest!

Never again, the chase he'll follow
By misty mount, or gloomy hollow;
Never be heard his sweet horn ringing,
Never his dogs' cry, gaily springing.

Never he'll urge his swift young steed,
Over the mound, and over the mead;
Change is o'er his fairness bowed,
O'er his glory fell a cloud.

O, generous Hand! thou'rt weak for aye!
Magnanimous Heart! thou art but clay!
Seed of knight, fast friend of the Bard,
O'er thee the spirits of song keep ward.

Bright Beam of Song! unquench'd thy fame,
My lay shall live with thy radiant name,
And win a tear in the after morrows
For thee, perchance, and thy Bard of sorrows.

THE FAIRIES.*
WILLIAM ALLINGHAM.
A Song for children.

Up the airy mountain,
  Down the rushy glen,
We daren't go a hunting
  For fear of little men;
Wee folk, good folk,
  Trooping all together;
Green jacket, red cap,
  And white owl's feather!

Down along the rocky shore
  Some make their home,
They live on crispy pan-cakes
  Of yellow tide foam;
Some in the reeds
  Of the black mountain-lake,
With frogs for their watch-dogs
  All night awake.

By the craggy hill-side,
  Through the mosses bare,
They have planted thorn-trees
  For pleasure here and there.
Is any man so daring
  To dig one up in spite?
He shall find the thornies set
  In his bed at night.

---

* The whole of this beautiful Song can be seen in Mr. Allingham's "Night and Day Songs;" we have given only a portion of it.

Up the airy mountain,
    Down the rushy glen,
We daren't go a hunting
    For fear of little men;
Wee folk, good folk,
    Trooping all together,
Green jacket, red cap,
    And white owl's feather!

THE "HOLLY AND IVY" GIRL.
KEEGAN.

[John Keegan, like Edward Walsh, was born of the people, and lived and died amongst them. He was born in the Queen's County in a village by the Nore, and died in the year 1849, at the age of forty years.]

" Come buy my nice, fresh Ivy, and my Hollysprigs so green;
I have the finest branches that ever yet were seen.
Come buy from me, good Christians, and let me home, I pray,
And I'll wish you, 'Merry Christmas Time,' and a ' Happy New Year's Day.'

Ah! won't you buy my Ivy?—the loveliest ever seen!
Ah! won't you buy my holly boughs?—all you who love the green!
Do!—take a little branch of each, and on my knees I'll pray,
That God may bless your Christmas, and be with your New Year's Day.

The wind is black and bitter, and the hailstones
  do not spare
My shivering form, my bleeding feet, and stiff
  entangled hair;
Then, when the skies are pitiless, be merciful I
  say—
So Heaven will light your Christmas and the
  coming New Year's Day."

—'Twas a dying maiden sung, while the cold hail
  rattled down,
And fierce winds whistled mournfully o'er Dublin's
  dreary town;—
One stiff hand clutched her Ivy-sprigs and Holly
  boughs so fair,
With the other she kept brushing the hail-drops
  from her hair.

So grim and statue-like she seemed, 'twas evident
  that Death
Was lurking in her footsteps—whilst her hot
  impeded breath
Too plainly told her early doom—though the
  burden of her lay
Was still of life, and Christmas joys, and a Happy
  New Year's Day.

'Twas in that broad bleak Thomas-Street, I heard
  the wanderer sing;
I stood a moment in the mire, beyond the ragged
  ring—
My heart felt cold and lonely, and my thoughts
  were far away,
Where I was, many a Christmas-tide, and Happy
  New Year's Day.

I dreamed of wanderings in the woods amongst
   the Holly Green;
I dreamed of my own native cot, and porch with
   Ivy screen;
I dreamed of lights for ever dimmed—of Hopes
   that can't return—
And dropped a tear on Christmas fires, that never
   more can burn.

The ghost-like singer still sung on, but no one
   came to buy;
The hurrying crowd passed to and fro, but did not
   heed her cry;
She uttered one low piercing moan—then cast her
   boughs away—
And smiling cried—" I'll rest with God before the
   New Year's Day!"

   *   *   *   *   *

On New Year's Day I said my prayers above a new-
   made grave,
Dug decently in sacred soil, by Liffey's murmur-
   ing wave;
The minstrel-maid from Earth to Heaven has winged
   her happy way,
And now enjoys with sister-saints, an endless New
   Year's Day.

THE SHAMROCK.
Ralph Varian.

When eager Spring sees Winter still
Fixed with his ice-belts on the hill ;
While leafless woods, all trembling, feel
The sap along their branches steal ;
And sheltered banks of mossy mould
Throw up the cups of white and gold ;
Though Winter, from the mountains yet
'Mid snow-sheets puffs his bitter breath ;
While Spring's fair breast with passion heaves—
I seek the Shamrock's triple leaves.

And when, from dewy mountain height,
She hangs her velvet mantle bright ;
And, drooping with laburnum-showers,
Looks through her lilac-scented bowers ;
While woods throw back her glittering beam,
With tender green and lucid gleam ;
While dance, to all her soft warm showers,
Her fragile, pensile, woodland flowers,
As Spring with deep'ning passion heaves—
I seek the Shamrock's triple leaves.

And when the beech with glittering mass
Of satin foliage sweeps the grass,
And June waves out her radiant wing
To dazzle sweet departing Spring ;
And foxglove-bells, and white-ray-flowers
Gleam through her shades of tangled bowers ;
And seas of fern heave and swell,
And stately moon-flowers fringe the dell,
And scarlet poppies nod, between
The fields of wheat, yet sappy green,

And trodden green sward breathing tells
Of clover white, with honey-cells;
And luscious blooms of golden vetch
To sea-shore meadows sunward stretch,
And Summer bathes in Spring's fresh Falls—
I seek the Shamrock's golden balls.

When flick'ring beams of golden hue
Through maples bathe germander blue,
And o'er the heaving meadow sod
The pearled and downy light stems nod,
Whose amber clusters drooping chime
Sweet greetings to the year's rich prime;
And great valerian reddens o'er
The walls of Ballintemple-shore;
And grass-plats of the gardens trim
With mignionette are blossoming,
And village doors and windows swing
To let the balm of summer in,
As latest shower from hawthorn falls—
I seek the Shamrock's golden balls.

When summer tempts the open boat,
Where breezes play and ripples float;
And, with vacation fully in,
Brings schoolboys to the river's rim;
While standing by the rugged way
The towering thistle eyes the day;
And crimson by the cottage walks,
Sweetwilliams glow and hollyhocks,
And sunflower—stately mystic flower—
Wheels with the slowly wheeling hour,
When panting Summer dries the Falls—
I seek the Shamrock's golden balls.

When Morning, with her eye of light,
Peers low among the branches bright,
And skimming on the sea-ward flow
Of winding river, swift or slow,
Sets Glanmire's steaming woods aglow;
And pennyroyal, flowering, lifts
His pale green wands, in fairy rifts;
And Autumn's crisp and glittering wings
Bring thoughts of Christmas-gatherings,
Bearing the fruited holly up,
Strewing the branch, and acorn cup,
Shaking the fragrant russets down,
With nuts upon her carpet brown;
From azure heights and orange halls
When latter rains fling waterfalls;
With clouds aglow, and breezes keen—
I seek the Shamrock's fadeless green,

When waterfowl, dejected, lag
By tall masts of the bulrush flag,
And rushy isle, with mist-wreath white,
Is centered in the gleaming light
Of frozen lough—a brilliant sight!
While ice-house hoards the frozen store,
And piled-up carts are bearing more;
And ice-men busy at the rim,
While skaters o'er the surface skim;
And by the cot and sheltered well,
The old thorn shows the icicle;
With snow in drifts and bright air keen,—
I seek the Shamrock's fadeless green.

When tired of day, pent up within,
And weary of the hammer's din;

Or shrinking from the creaking hinge,
As rich men flaunt and poor men cringe ;
Or 'mid their halls, my spirit palls
At bigot-creeds, and party calls ;
Or tightened brow begins to fade,
Ere evening spreads her twilight shade ;
Ere stars arise, ere sunsets fall,
'Mid Autumn-dyes, or Spring's fresh call,
Or barren Winter, leafless grieves—
I seek the Shamrock's triple leaves.

MY VIOLON.
By Thomas Irwin.

Within my little lonely room
  Where many a crimson evening shines,
I cheer away the falling gloom
  With songs beneath the casement-vines :
    Sweet memories haunt the lingering day
    That hovers o'er each golden sun—
      Each tune I play
      Brings back a ray—
    Sing to me, sing, old Violon.

Old friends, your homes in sunset shine,
  The trees around them softly sigh,
While o'er the rolling distant brine
  You sail from home and poverty ;
    I see your vessel far away,
    I see your faces sad and wan
      Turned where the day
      Sets wild and grey—
    Sing to them, sing, old Violon.

Old books—companions of my youth,
  And friends of age still brightening earth,
How oft we've mused above your truth,
  How often smiled upon your mirth!
Your date recalls the happy years
    And all who blessed them passed and gone—
      Their smile appears
      'Mid falling tears—
Sing to them, sing, old Violon!

Companionless amid the days
  I wander in the Autumn blast,
Through fields and trees, and well-known ways,
  The silent scenery of the past.
Like friends the distant mountains smile
    O'erflowed by the departing sun—
      A little while,
      A little while,
Sing to them yet, old Violon.

Yon pale autumnal cloud of white
  Stood in the cold east all day long,
And in the silent sky to-night
  Under the full moon hears my song.
My fancy whispers mournfully—
    'Tis some dear spirit beloved and gone,
      Come back to see
      Old earth and me—
Sing to her, sing, old Violon.

Ah! soon, sweet friend, thy aged strings
  To stranger fingers shall resound;
But, when to thy rich murmurings
  The joyous dancers beat the ground,

Through the gay window with the moon
    I'll look ere mirth and dance be done,
      And list thy tune,
      Though soon, too soon
Death wafts me from my Violon.

THE BLACKSMITH OF LIMERICK.
Robert Dwyer Joyce.

He grasped his ponderous hammer, he could not stand it more,
To hear the bombshells bursting, and thundering battle's roar;
He said—"The breach they're mounting, the Dutchman's murdering crew—
I'll try my hammer on their heads and see what *that* can do!

"Now swarthy Ned and Moran, make up that iron well;
'Tis Sarsfield's horse that wants the shoes, so mind not shot or shell!"
"Ah sure," cried both, "the horse can wait—for Sarsfield's on the wall,
And where you go we'll follow, with you to stand or fall!"

The blacksmith raised his hammer, and rushed into the street,
His 'prentice boys behind him, the ruthless foe to meet—
High on the breach of Limerick, with dauntless hearts they stood,
Where the bombshells burst, and shot fell thick, and redly ran the blood.

"Now look you, brown-haired Moran, and mark
  you, swarthy Ned,
This day we'll prove the thickness of many a
  Dutchman's head!
Hurra! upon their bloody path they're mounting
  gallantly;
And now, the first that tops the breach, leave him
  to this and me!"

The first that gained the rampart, he was a captain
  brave,
A captain of the grenadiers, with blood-stained dirk
  and glaive;
He pointed and he parried, but it was all in vain,
For fast thro' skull and helmet the hammer found
  his brain!

The next that topt the rampart, he was a colonel
  bold,
Bright thro' the murk of battle his helmet flashed
  with gold—
"Gold is no match for iron!" the doughty blacksmith
  said,
As with that ponderous hammer he cracked his
  foeman's head!

"Hurra for gallant Limerick!" black Ned and Moran
  cried,
As on the Dutchmen's leaden heads their hammers
  well they plied;
A bombshell burst between them—one fell without a groan,
One leapt into the lurid air, and down the breach
  was thrown!

"Brave smith! brave smith!" cried Sarsfield,
  " beware the treacherous mine —
Brave smith! brave smith! fall backward, or surely
  death is thine!"
The smith sprang up the rampart, and leaped the
  blood-stained wall,
As high into the shuddering air went foemen, breach,
  and all!

Up like a red volcano they thundered wild and high,
Spear, gun, and shattered standard, and foemen
  thro' the sky;
And dark and bloody was the shower that round
  the blacksmith fell—
He thought upon his 'prentice boys, they were
  avengèd well!

On foemen and defenders a silence gathered down
'Twas broken by a triumph-shout that shook the
  ancient town;
As out its heroes sallied, and bravely charged and
  slew,
And taught King William and his men what Irish
  hearts can do!

Down rushed the swarthy blacksmith unto the river
  side,
He hammered on the foe's pontoon, to sink it in
  the tide;
The timber it was tough and strong, it took no crack
  or strain—
"Mavrone, 'twon't break," the blacksmith roared,
  " I'll try their heads again!"

* * * * * * *

The blacksmith sought his smithy, and blew his
   bellows strong,
He shod the steed of Sarsfield, but o'er it sang
   no song;
"Ochón! my boys are dead," he cried; "their
   loss I'll long deplore,
But comfort's in my heart, their graves are red with
   foreign gore!"

GENTLE BRIDEEN.
(From the Irish of O'Carolan.)
GEORGE SIGERSON—TRANSLATOR.
"A brıgıtt nıc uı Майlе ıт ɼu ɒ'ꝼas mo ċɼoıɓte
   cɼaıɓte."

Fair Brideen O'Malley, thou'st left me in sadness,
   My bosom is pierced with Love's arrows so keen,
For thy mien it is graceful, thy glances are gladness,
   And thousands thy lovers, O gentle Brideen!

The grey mists of morning in autumn were fleeting,
   When I met the bright darling—down in the
      boreen;
Her words were unkind, but I soon won a greeting,
   Sweet kisses I stole from the lips of Brideen!

O! fair is the sun in the dawning all tender,
   And beauteous the roses beneath it are seen,
Thy cheek is the red rose! Thy brow the sun-splen-
      dour!
   And, Cluster of ringlets! my dawn is Brideen!

Then shine, O bright Sun, on thy constant, true lover,
Then shine, once again, in the leafy boreen,
And the clouds shall depart that around my heart hover.
And we'll walk amid gladness, my gentle Brideen!

ON THE BAY.
Boat Song:—Glengariffe.
Ralph Varian.

Moonlight follows glowing day—
Launch the boat upon the bay;
Play the oars with timely zest,
Gently on Glengariffe's breast.

All things bright and lovely here,
Wake the smile and start the tear;
Mountain sprites through valleys float,
Catch the trembling bugle-note.

Glorious mountains, piled around,
Shelter the enchanted ground;
Mirror, struck by pliant oar,
Gold showers to the woodland shore.

Place the helm in fairest hands,
Bear the boat to silver sands;
Mingawn-Buidhe,* and pigeon cave,
Shadowed in the moon-lit wave.

* Mingawn Buidhe (pr: *bwee*) and Pigeon Cave—both are situated outside the Bay, at Pooleen Cove: the cave is remarkable: the cliffs are magnificent. Mingawn Buidhe—"The Yellow Kid Rock." Here too are "The Seal Caves."

As we glide o'er sheltered deeps,
In this glen, where ocean sleeps,
'Neath the pale moon's placid ray,
And the stars that gem the Bay:

Raise the song for those who rest,
Banished from Glengariffe's breast,
In New World, by primal trees,
Or in far Antipodes.

" Oars that move their boats afar,
Work beneath propitious star ;
Shadowy tides of life, when struck,
Splendours yield to their true work :

" May their souls, with rays divine,
Still round Erinn's glories shine ;
And their hearts to ours keep time,
Circling in a distant clime.

" Beaming to Glengariffe's shore,
Where we ply the steady oar ;
And the green star sheds its rays,
Herald of triumphant days."
   Play the oars with timely rest,
   Gently on Glengariffe's breast.

ROVING BRIAN O'CONNELL.
ROBERT DWYER JOYCE.
AIR.—"How do you like her for your wife."

"How do you like her for your wife,
  Roving Brian O'Connell?
A loving mate and true for life,
  Roving Brian O'Connell?"
"She's as fit to be my wife
As my sword is for the strife,"
Said the Rapparee trooper,
  Roving Brian O'Connell!

"Ne'er to Mabel prove untrue,
  Roving Brian O'Connell,
For oh! she'd die for love of you
  Roving Brian O'Connell!"
"Oh! my wild heart never knew
A flame so constant too,"
Said the Rapparee trooper,
  Roving Brian O'Connell!

"Her father died, as dies the brave,
  Roving Brian O'Connell,
Beneath the blow the Saxon gave,
  Roving Brian O'Connell."
"Next we'll meet the Saxon knave
He'll get pike and gun and glaive!"
Said the Rapparee trooper,
  Roving Brian O'Connell.

"How will you your young bride keep,
  Roving Brian O'Connell?
The Foeman's bands are ne'er asleep,
  Roving Brian O'Connell."

"In our hold by Conail's steep
Who dare make my Mabel weep?"
Said the Rapparee trooper,
   Roving Brian O'Connell.

"This day in ruined church you stand,
   Roving Brian O'Connell,
To take your young bride's priceless hand,
   Roving Brian O'Connell."
Oh, my heart, my arm, my brand,
Are for her and our dear land!"
Said the Rapparee trooper,
   Roving Brian O'Connell!

AN IRISH MOTHER'S DREAM.
Thomas Irwin.*

One night, as the wind of the Winter blew loud,
And snow wreathed the earth like a corse in its shroud,
  An aged mother mused in her dim cottage shed,
    O'er the young soldier-son of her heart far away,
  Where the cannon flames red o'er the low lying dead,
    And the desolate camp bleakly spreads in the day.
  And near stood her Daughter, with sad strainéd smile,
    And kind cheek of care, that long weeping had worn,
As she whispered: "Now sleep, dearest Mother, awhile—
   God is good, and our Dermot will surely return."

The poor Mother turned on her pillow, and there
Soon slept the kind sleep Heaven sheds on our care.
  Silence filled the dusk chamber—the low ashy
    hearth
  Sunk lower, and noiselessly sifted the snow
O'er the white spacious girth of the cold, solemn
    earth,
    Where the muffled moon fitfully glimmered
    below ;
But vanished awhile are her visions of fear,
    And passed, for a space, is her sorrow and
    pain ;
For an angel has wafted her soul from its sphere,
    And in dreams she beholds her own Dermot
    again.

Dear joy, how she loves him! A long year has passed
Since she kissed his pale forehead, and hung on
    his breast ;
  She looks in his face—'tis the same, still the
    same—
  Still soft are those eyes as the dew on the sod:
No thirst for the game of wild battle or fame
    Have lessened their love for her, thanks be
    to God!
But away! they are speeding o'er mountain and
    moor—
  O'er city, and forest—o'er tempest and tide ;
But little she heeds of their terrors, be sure,
    While that son of her bosom seems still by
    her side.

* Of Dublin—Author of a volume of excellent poems entitled " Versicles," published by The " Celtic Union."

Lo ! at length they have passed the wild ocean, and
    stand
On a summit that looks o'er a desolate land ;
  Far off, the great fortresses boom o'er the spray,
    Anear, the black tents drift the slopes of the
      ground ;
  And a sense of decay fills the solitude gray,
    For an army in ruins is scattered around.
  " And is it for this," said the poor dreaming soul,
    " My Dermot has wandered from home's
      blessed air ?—
  Here Death fills the wind blowing keen from the
      Pole—
    Here the Pestilence strikes what the cannon
      may spare."

They passed through the streets of the tents lying
    still—
They passed through the trenches that ridge the
    brown hill—
  They saw the pale faces that famine has worn ;
    They pace where the wounded lie lonely and
      lost—
  Where the corse, cannon-torn, to its red bed
      was borne—
    Where the poor frozen sentinel died on his
      post.
  " Ah, why, Dermot, why did you cross the wide
      foam,
    To fortune, my child, in this land of the dead ?
  Sure we'd plenty at home—there was better to
      come :
    Why, for this, did you leave me, acushla?" she
      said.

"I thought as you grew fond and brave by my side,
No sorrow could cloud us—no fate could divide;
　I fancied the day when our home would grow
　　bright,
　　With the smile of some *coleen* I'd cherish for
　　　thee —
　When I'd sing through the night by the hearth's
　　ruddy light,
　　With your boy, my own Dermot, asleep on
　　　my knee;
And when, circled round by a few happy friends,
　Old age drooped my head after many a year,
As I passed to my God, through the death that
　he sends,
　　The kind Father would bless me, and you
　　　would be near."

Still close in the gloom seems he standing by her;
But hark! 'tis the drum, and the camp is astir;
　And a sound fills the air, from the hill to the star,
　　Like an earthquake along the wild bastion it
　　　runs,
　While echoes afar roar the voice of the War,
　　As it doubles its thunders from thousands of
　　　guns,
　And she wakes. In the gleam of the pale
　　morning air
　　One gives her a letter—soon, soon it is read;
But a low piteous moan only speaks her despair—
　"Ah, Mother of God! my own Dermot is dead!"

THE LUPRACAUN, OR FAIRY SHOEMAKER:
(A rhyme for children.)
WILLIAM ALLINGHAM.

Little Cowboy, what have you heard,
  Up on the lonely rath's green mound?
Only the plaintive yellow bird
  Sighing in sultry fields around,
Charry, charry, charry, chee-e !
Only the grasshopper and the bee?
  " Tip-tap, rip-rap,
    Tick-a-tack-too !
  Scarlet leather sewn together,
    This will make a shoe.
  Left, right, pull it tight;
    Summer days are warm ;
  Underground, in winter,
    Laughing at the storm !"
Lay your ear close to the hill.
Do you not catch the tiny clamour;
Busy click of an elfin hammer,
Voice of the Lupracaun singing shrill
  As he merrily plies his trade?
    He's a span
    And a quarter in height.
Get him in sight, hold him fast,
    And you're a made
      Man !

You watch your cattle the summer day,
Sup on potatoes, sleep in the hay ;
  How should you like to roll in your carriage,
  And look for a duchess's daughter in marriage?
Seize the Shoemaker—so you may !

"Big boots a hunting,
  Sandals in the hall,
White for a wedding feast,
  And pink for a ball.
This way, that way,
  So we make a shoe,
Getting rich every stitch,
  Tick-tack-too!
Nine and ninety treasure-crocks
This keen miser-fairy hath,
Hid in mountain, wood, and rocks,
Ruin and round-tower, cave and rath,
  And where the cormorants build;
    From times of old
    Guarded by him;
    Each of them filled
    Full to the brim
      With gold!

I caught him at work one day, myself,
  In the castle-ditch where the foxglove grows;
A wrinkled, wizened, and bearded elf,
  Spectacles stuck on the point of his nose,
Silver buckles to his hose,
  Leather apron—shoe in his lap—
    "Rip-rap, tip-tap,
      Tack-tack-too!
    A grig skipped upon my cap,
      Away the moth flew.
    Buskins for a fairy prince,
      Brogues for his son,—
    Pay me well, pay me well,
      When the job is done!"

The rogue was mine, beyond a doubt.
I stared at him; he stared at me;
" Servant, sir!" " Humph!" says he,
   And pulled a snuffbox out.
He took a long pinch, looked better pleased,
   The queer little Lupracaun;
Offered the box with a whimsical grace,—
Pouf! he flung the dust in my face,
   And, while I sneezed,
      Was gone!

MALLOW.
Ralph Varian.

Where woods and lawns retiring slope,
I found my life, my health, my hope—
A well of Love that dimples o'er,
And that is—Mairé geal mo stor.*

The Mallow Well springs bubbling up
Where feeble hearts drink living hope—
Your smile the dying would restore,
My gentle Maire geal mo stor.

Where rivers flow between the hills,
In honey-vales, by flowery rills—
Her fame—they sing it o'er and o'er—
The fame of Maire geal mo stor.

Around The Ring of Mallow town,
When flowers were high and corn down,
And brown leaves still, and hounds astir,
I met with Maire geal mo stor.

  * Mauria gal mostore: bright Mary, treasure.

The Lee, and Bride 'mid shadows beam,
Where woods retire, and pastures gleam!
But Heaven wreathes the crystal floor,
That murmurs round my Maire's door.

Old Munster's streams are fair to see;
The Suir, the Shannon, and the Lee;
There, too, the Blackwater can pour
Its murmurs round my Maire's door.

Give me the form, the russet gown,
The dimples fair, the apples brown,
The sunny smile, the playful stir
Of gentle Maire geal mo stor.

Take wealth, and rank, and rustling sweep
Of silken gown, on carpets deep;
Give me a cot, a frugal store,
And gentle Maire geal mo stor.

UP!
A VERNAL ODE.
Street Song: written in 1798.

'Tis Spring, and blithe from spray to spray
 The winged musicians hop,
Uniting in a roundelay,
 As if they all were UP.

Each plants erects its pendent head,
 Each flower expands its cup;
The very weeds in every bed
 Set impudently UP.

There's not a tree in wood or grove
 That waves its branchy top,
Which does not hoist the badge of love
 And union, boldly UP.

The brambles on the highway side,
    A numerous, hardy crop,
So long kept down by winter's pride,
    Spring amicably UP.

The tenants of the crystal stream
    Their heads above it pop!
As if they wanted to exclaim,
    " See, Neighbours, we are UP."

Each hill now cocks its crest on high
    As any martial fop,
While every valley seems to cry,
    " Come down and help us UP."

The progress of this rising rage,
    No human power can stop—
Then Tyrants cease your war to wage,
    For NATURE WILL BE UP.

OVER THE MORNING DEW.
ROBERT DWYER JOYCE.

AIR—" *As truagh gan peata vier agum.*"

It is the sweetest hour of love:
The sun is o'er the eastern grove,
And nought is heard but coo of dove,
    And wild streams in the greenwood :—
Over the morning dew,
Over the morning dew,
Come with me, young gradh mo chroide,*
    Unto the leafy greenwood!

  * Grau mo chree: love of my heart.

With flowers that bloom so sweetly there
I'll deck thy dress and golden hair,
And thou hast never looked so fair,
 As there in that wild greenwood :—
Over the morning dew,
Over the morning dew,
Come with me, young gradh mo chroide,
 Unto the leafy greenwood !

There rears the Rath its lonely height,
Where fairies come at noon of night,
And there my faith I'll fondly plight
 To thee in that wild greenwood !
Over the morning dew,
Over the morning dew,
Come with me, young gradh mo chroide,
 Unto the leafy greenwood !

Oh ! fear not here to stray with me ;
You know me from your infancy ;
I'll ask but look of love from thee,
 And fond kiss in the greenwood.
Over the morning dew,
Over the morning dew,
Then come with me, young gradh mo chroide,
 Unto the leafy greenwood !

TIME'S EARTHQUAKE.

T. Irwin.

Lo ! the elements gathered for ages, unroll,
Their thunder-clouds bursting from tropic to pole!—
Let the storm speed amain—yon red star in the sky
Proclaims that the earthquake of Nations is nigh.
Change quickens the world : from its dawn overcast,
Eternity's bell tolls the hour from the vast,
Where regenerant chaos out-spreading its wings
Shall roll to their ruin the Empires, the Kings—
While the slumbering giant Democracies, bound,
By diplomatists' Lilliput-chains to the ground,
With an upheaving stretch of their gaunt giant
    bones,
Shake to air the dynastic dominion of Thrones.—
Let it come, let it come ; richer æon will rise
When the war-smoke drifts off from the purified
    skies :
Then may Peace, pacing on from the clear golden
    morn,
Weed the world of its tares, scatter dew on its corn,
Set a heavenlier star on the brow of the Age,
Arm for noblest battle Saint, Hero and Sage ;
While the nations reshaped by the earthquake of
    Time
Independent and equal, secure and sublime,
Round the old rolling world a new lustre may fling,
Like the strong solid splendour of Saturn's great
    ring,
Still brightening as through the vast cycles they run,
In the civilized glories of Liberty's sun !

THE HEATHER GLEN,

AN ULSTER SONG.

GEORGE SIGERSON.

AIR.—"An Smacteen Cron."*

There blooms a bonnie flower
  Up the heather glenn,
Though bright in sun,—in shower
  'Tis just as bright again !
I never *can* pass by it—
I never dar' go nigh it—
My heart it won't be quiet
  Up the heather glenn !

    Sing O, the blooming heather !
      O, the heather glenn !
    Where fairest fairies gather
      To lure in mortal men !
    I never can pass by it—
    I never dar' go nigh it—
    My heart it won't be quiet
      Up the heather glenn !

There sings a bonnie linnet
  Up the heather glenn,
The voice has magic in it
  Too sweet for mortal men !
It brings Joy down before us
Wi' winsome mellow chorus,
But flies—far, too far, o'er us
  Up the heather glenn !

---

* The music of this air is to be found in the first series of "Poets of Munster," published by O'Daly, Dublin.

Sing, O, the blooming heather!
  O, the heather glenn!
Where fairest fairies gather
  To lure in mortal men!
I never can pass by it—
I never dar' go nigh it—
My heart it won't be quiet
  Up the heather glenn!

O, might I pull the flower
  That's blooming in that glenn,
Nae sorrow that could lower,
  Would make me sad again!
And might I catch that linnet;
My heart—my hope are in it!
O, heaven itself I'd win it
  Up the heather glenn!

Sing, O, the blooming heather!
  O, the heather glenn!
Where fairest fairies gather
  To lure in mortal men!
I never can pass by it—
I never dar' go nigh it—
My heart it won't be quiet
  Up the heather glenn!

TO AN INFANT.

ON PRESENTING HER WITH A GREEN TOP-KNOT ON HER BIRTH-DAY.

From "The Press" Newspaper, October 12th, 1797.
ANONYMOUS.

Sweet were her infant smiles, and sweet her mien,
As on her brow I bound the Ribbon Green ;
For nature's child should nature's livery wear,
And Green is the banner Erinn's sons should bear.
Her daughters, too, should verdant fillets grace,
And next their hearts the mystic shamrock place.
Green are her fields, her waves, and green each grove,
And green is the badge of liberty and love.
The myrtle green is heaven's favourite tree,
First planted in the land of liberty.
O, favourite Isle, by Nature truly blessed,
Too long insulted and too long oppressed ;
Though once the seat of Arts and ancient lore,
Thy learning and thy arts are seen no more ;
Though on thy soil, no poisonous reptile lives,
Thy fruits to foreign slaves profuse it gives ;
A venal vermin servilely sustains ;
Poor Erinn long has felt sore galling chains,
And God who raised her high above the wave,
And made her daughters fair,—their brothers brave;
Her shores protected by the circling flood,
Blessed the green Isle, and said that it was good.
May heaven, propitious, hear my anxious vow,
And bless the charm that binds thy fairy brow ;—
Make her the mother of a hardy race,—
Thy sons give freedom, and thy daughters peace.

THE SHEPHERD'S FAREWELL.
Translated from the Spanish of Villanueva,
BY GEORGE SIGERSON.

Ballyshannon, flowery village,
Flowery village, once my home!
Peaceful rest among thy mountains
That afar off see me roam.
   Left my little flock for ever;
Never by the river-tide
Shall I tend the merry kidling
Leaping by its mother's side—
On the upland pasture, never
Pass the glowing noon away,
Shaded 'neath the wavering wild rose
Looking o'er the dreamy bay.
Bear I these alone for dower,—
Flowery village, once my home!—
Sweet old tunes and songs of childhood
   In my breast, where'er I roam.

On this mountain slope above thee
Where I spent my happy time,
'Mid the fruit my hands had planted
Gladdened by thy distant chime,
   Here, ere leaving thee for ever
Here, I light a fire,—the last,
'Mid my cot's down-broken ruins
And the ruins of the Past.
Nought remains of all my labour—
Nought but broom and nettle rank,
Thistle, gorse and wild weed cluster
Over meadowy field and bank.

Burst in flames, dry wood and bramble!
Light the ruins of my home,
And the sad steps of its master
   Who afar off now must roam.

Seeking some fair spot of safety
O'er the hills my path shall lie,
Sleeping, mayhap, in their bosoms
'Neath the vigil of the sky—
   Sleeping mayhaps, by the fireside
Of some shepherd, rough and kind,
With my heart gone back in slumber
To the land I left behind,
Or it may be, in the valleys
Wander through the gentle Spring,
Tilling 'mid the lowland gardens,
While green leaves are opening;
Or, upon the moving waters
Seek the good gifts of the sea,
Till another tempest coming
   Drive me off, as now from thee.

But amid the cities never—
Never shall my pathway lie,
Where great walls shut out the mountains
And dark smoke the holy sky.
Ballyshannon, flowery village,
Flowery village, once my home!
Peaceful rest among thy mountains
That afar off see me roam.

THE END.

www.ingramcontent.com/pod-product-compliance
Lightning Source LLC
Chambersburg PA
CBHW030403250426
43670CB00050B/439